Fox Talbot

Martin Andrews was, for many years, a museum and exhibition designer and a member of staff at the Museum of Reading. In 1990 he became a lecturer in the Department of Typography & Graphic Communication at the University of Reading. More recently he has concentrated on printing and design history; he has published numerous articles on the subject and lectured extensively in the UK and abroad. His biography of the artist, author and adventurer Robert Gibbings was published in 2003. In retirement, Martin is pursuing a new career as an artist, illustrator and writer.

Opposite:
Printed by John Snare, Reading
A Selection of Specimens of the Talbotype or Sun Pictures
Letterpress broadside, probably 1846
44.5 × 28.8 cm

FOX TALBOT
& the Reading Establishment

Written and illustrated by
Martin Andrews

TWO
RIVERS
PRESS

First published in the UK in 2014 by Two Rivers Press
7 Denmark Road, Reading RG1 5PA
www.tworiverspress.com

ISBN 978-1-901677-98-0

1 2 3 4 5 6 7 8 9

Two Rivers Press is represented in the UK by Inpress Ltd and
distributed by Central Books.

Illustrations by Martin Andrews
Cover and text design by Nadja Guggi
Typeset in Bembo and Parisine

Printed and bound in Great Britain by Ashford Colour Press, Gosport

To Oliver George Hepburn, a young historian in the making

Acknowledgements

The writing and publication of this small history would not have been possible without the support, advice and help of friends, colleagues and institutions.

I would like to thank my wife, Verity, for her patience and for reading very rough drafts; Two Rivers Press for making this book possible; Anke Ueberberg for her meticulous editing and Nadja Guggi for her wonderful design; Roger Watson, the curator at the Fox Talbot Museum at Lacock, for his invaluable advice; Sidney Gold for providing so much knowledge of local history and to Evelyn Williams for providing information on Cowderoy; James Watkins for commenting on drafts; Alan Hardie for helping with research; Alexandra Martin for her research and providing the initial idea for the book; Adam Sowan for his specialist knowledge of the Great Western Railway, and Adam and Barbara Morris for reading the proofs; Reading Local Studies Library for use of their source material and permission to reproduce Talbot's photographs of Reading; Professor Larry Schaaf and the University of Glasgow for permission to quote extensively from Talbot's correspondence; Hans P. Kraus Jr., New York, for kind permission to reproduce the John Snare poster on the inside front cover; and Lesley Saunders for her poem.

Contents

Introduction

My purpose in writing this short history is to celebrate an important episode in Reading's history of which the public is generally not aware. This book is not an academic study of photography but an attempt to bring alive events and personalities in the context of location and time: the town of Reading in the 1840s.

The title of the book features the name of William Henry Fox Talbot, the famous pioneer photographer, but it would be equally appropriate to call it *Nicolaas Henneman and the Reading Establishment*. The reader will discover that much of what follows is concerned with the achievements of Henneman, Talbot's former valet and photographic assistant. Sadly, he fell into obscurity in later life, and his name is little known by most people today. So, in part, another purpose of this book is to acknowledge Henneman's contribution to the development of photography.

Before we begin our account of the Reading Establishment, I must clarify some issues of terminology.

In the text I have referred to William Henry Fox Talbot as 'Talbot' for brevity. 'Fox Talbot' appears in the title of this book for the sake of recognition, but there is some suggestion that Talbot disliked using his given name 'Fox'.

The business that Talbot and Henneman set up in Reading was not officially called 'The Reading Establishment', but the phrase appears in notes written by Benjamin Cowderoy in 1846. The name stuck and generally refers to the photographic studio. For convenience, I have used it throughout the book.

Another term that is in everyday use today but might not have been used by Talbot and Henneman in the 1840s is 'photograph'. It was coined in 1839 by Sir John Herschel, a fellow scientist and friend of Talbot's, although in France the term 'photographie' had possibly come into use a few years earlier. Talbot and Henneman would have called photographic prints 'sun pictures', Talbotypes or calotypes, but 'photograph' is universally understood today so I have adopted it from the start. Herschel also introduced the terms 'negative' and 'positive'.

Finally, I have quoted extensively from the letters of Nicolaas Henneman, retaining their remarkable spelling and punctuation – be warned.

The Reading Establishment only operated for just over three years, but its significance in the development of photography is great – and it all happened in Reading. So now, dear reader, read on…

A mysterious gentleman

The year is 1843. Dickens is working on *A Christmas Carol* for publication later in the year to capture the seasonal market. In June, Parliament passes a Factory Act fixing the working day to twelve hours for women and to six hours for children aged between eight and thirteen years of age. On 19 July, Isambard Kingdom Brunel witnesses Prince Albert launching the SS *Great Britain*, the world's first screw-propelled iron transatlantic liner. In the Berkshire market town of Reading the gossip is about the appearance of a mysterious foreign stranger.

This elusive gentleman particularly fascinates two young apprentices. They are chatting away, hidden in the labyrinth of bookshelves in Lovejoy's subscription library in London Street, while their employer, George Lovejoy, of Pickwickian appearance with his round face, small glasses perched on the end of his nose, unruly hair and a mischievous glint in his eye, engages one of his literary friends in lively conversation. The apprentices' speculation is getting rather out of hand: people are saying he is a forger of bank notes – could they be right?

As an elderly man in 1898, one of these two young men wrote down his memories of these events. His name was John Henderson, his friend's was Alfred Harrison, and they had both met the mysterious stranger when they served him in the stationery department of the bookshop at the front of the library:

> Reading was a comparatively small Town at that time, and any new resident was sure to cause some attention, especially if a Foreigner; his consistent visits to our shop, where he purchased every kind of writing paper we could supply, and then going direct to a well known Chemist for various chemicals not in general use, soon aroused suspicion as to his vocation; he lived alone with an old housekeeper in a tolerably good house which had been a School, where there was a large room without windows, but a skylight in the play ground; this

he used for his experiments, and always kept securely locked; prying neighbours and others who made inquiries about him soon came to the conclusion that he was engaged in forging Foreign Bank Notes or some such nefarious pursuit. My fellow apprentice, Harrison, & myself were often questioned as to what we knew about him, but for a long time he kept his own counsel and we were all in the dark.

... his house-keeper thought he was a most mysterious person, his hands being stained all shades from brown to black; he never appeared in public unless well gloved...

The truth behind these rumours was far less sensational than the good citizens of Reading speculated – but no less significant. The gentleman who aroused so much suspicion was a Dutchman called Nicolaas Henneman who, until recently, had been employed by William Henry Fox Talbot, the great pioneer in the invention and development of photography. Henneman was financially supported by Talbot to set up a commercial photographic studio and processing laboratory in Reading – the first of its kind – which has come to be referred to as the 'Reading Establishment'. Here, over the next few years, they would produce the first book in the world to be illustrated by photographs – a momentous publication that was to mark a huge change in visual communication and the way we view the world.

The impact of photography can be seen in many areas of human activity – science and technology, the arts, journalism, education, documentation, advertising and marketing, social interaction and leisure – and today it is an intrinsic part of our lives. It was not always so; before photography, a visual record of our world could only be captured by the artist. Images could be duplicated and distributed through printing but these images had to be conveyed through the artificial construction of marks made by tools carving in wood, incising into metal plates or by drawing in greasy crayon on stone. In each case our view of the world was filtered through the eyes of the artist and the handiwork of the technician who made the printing surface. With photography came a new realism: for the first time images were a direct recording of the world around us, free from the interpretation and translation of the artist's hand. Suddenly people could have a record of what they looked like and see images of far-away places, cultures and and events as if they had been there themselves – it seemed like a new truth.

The photographic image has become a central part of our everyday lives and plays a crucial role in modern society – and an important step in this revolutionary development took place in Reading.

Before we delve into the story of the 'Reading Establishment' it might help our understanding of the events that follow if we briefly look at the invention of photography itself.

The birth of photography

Many of us have only a rudimentary knowledge of optics and chemistry so this account of the birth and development of photography will be brief and try not to bemuse the reader with a plethora of technical detail that has already been comprehensively covered elsewhere. Besides, at its heart, the story of photography is a human story of rivalry, ambition, the desire for financial gain and the frustrated attempts of amateur artists to depict the world around them. This latter point will need explaining, but let us start with the idea that photography relies on bringing together two sciences – optics and chemistry.

How many humans, from the earliest times, have wanted to freeze and capture their fleeting image reflected on water or in a mirror? Another phenomenon through which we experience a reflection of the world around us had also been known since ancient time: the classical philosopher Aristotle described it in the fourth century BC and perhaps you have observed it when lying in bed during the day with the curtains closed. In a blacked-out room, a chink of light passing through a tiny gap or hole in the drawn curtains will throw a miniature image of the view outside, reflected by the light of the sun, onto the wall opposite the window – but upside down. The

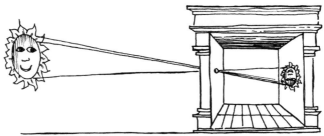

Sic nos exactè Anno .1544 . Louanii eclipsim Solis

Camera obscura or dark room

smaller the hole, the sharper the image will be. The principle of this optical effect was well known to Arabian scholars, and a man called Alhazen described it in a book on optics in the eleventh century. Rooms especially designed to produce this phenomenon were built to observe solar eclipses while avoiding damage to the eyes. Such devices were given the name 'camera obscura', from the Latin for 'dark room'.

Leonardo da Vinci's notebooks contain two descriptions of the camera obscura, and in 1558 another Italian, Giovanni Battista della Porta, wrote a very detailed description of the device and recommended it as an aid to artists, suggesting that they could trace the reflected image onto paper as a basis for a painting. It is thought that the great Dutch painter of interiors, Vermeer, installed a camera obscura in his house in the middle of the seventeenth century, and in the next century Canaletto, famous for his detailed views of cities, made frequent use of the device. Joshua Reynolds owned a camera obscura that was

Model: I can't wait for the <u>reflex</u> camera obscura

disguised as a book. In recent times, the artist David Hockney became fascinated by its potential and has written about its historical impact as a tool for painters.

By the middle of the sixteenth century the brightness and intensity of the projected image was improved by the introduction of a lens into the aperture. However, the restrictions created by the necessity of a darkened room were a problem, and numerous eccentric attempts were made to construct collapsible, portable 'rooms'. A simple, practical solution was found in the seventeenth century in the form of a wooden box with an aperture for the lens at the front and a waxed paper screen (later a ground glass screen) at the back to hold the image. This allowed the camera obscura to be easily handled and portable. To see the image on the screen it was necessary to view it under cover of a black cloth at the back of the camera.

The problem of the inverted image was overcome by the concept of the reflex camera, introduced at the end of the sixteenth century. By placing a mirror at the back of the box at 45 degrees to the lens, the image could be reflected up onto a screen the right way round – using the same principle as

Table camera obscura, c. 1769

Nineteenth-century reflex camera obscura

the single lens reflex camera (SLR) today. The camera obscura could also be made to any size, down to a pocket version.

Now anyone could make accurate perspective drawings, even if they lacked artistic talent. It became a fashion amongst the wealthy classes as an entertainment. Ladies and gentlemen of leisure delighted in this new-fangled technology. Weird and wonderful designs were thought up – sedan chairs and horse-drawn carriages were adapted for the purpose and extending table camera obscuras, fashioned using the latest styles in cabinet making, became desirable adornments for the sitting room or library. Of course there were many more serious applications too, particularly in the field of surveying.

The 'darkened room' form of the camera obscura lives on as a fascinating spectacle for the public. It became an entertainment and a tourist attraction in the nineteenth century and camera obscuras were built in many cities, often at the top of a tower, to provide panoramic views. Edinburgh's camera obscura is still in use today and remains a popular visitor attraction. Aberystwyth boasts that its camera obscura at the top of the electric Cliff Railway is the biggest in the world still in operation.

In essence, the hand-held camera obscura was the precursor of the modern camera; however, it was developments in chemistry that provided the next essential ingredient to make the invention of photography possible.

The optical aspect of capturing an image had been solved by the camera obscura but how to permanently fix that elusive image drawn with light on the screen of the camera was still a mystery. From ancient times alchemists had been experimenting with chemistry and discovered useful preparations such as nitrate of silver and chloride of silver, often by accident. In the sixteenth century the darkening of silver compounds on exposure to light was noted, and other effects of sunlight were well known – the bleaching of fabrics and the tanning of skin – but the cause was not understood.

It was not until 1725 that Johann Heinrich Schulze, a professor of anatomy at a university near Nuremberg, made a vital discovery. Schulze was experimenting in his laboratory with a chalky solution that happened to contain silver nitrate. When he put the flask containing the solution next to the window he noticed that the solution on the side exposed to the sun had darkened to a purple colour, whereas on the opposite side it remained unchanged. He realised that this was the effect of  light rather than the heat of the sun or exposure to air, as had previously been thought. He then had the idea of cutting letters and silhouettes of little figures out of a piece of paper to form a stencil; he wrapped this around the

Johann Heinrich Schulze (1687–1744)

flask and exposed the solution to light again. After a while the light passing through the stencil darkened the cloudy solution – 'printing' the words and images on the liquid as if by magic. He showed this trick to his astonished friends and it soon became a fashionable and popular party piece, but in fact, it was a serious discovery – he had found a way to demonstrate that the light of the sun could be imprinted using chemistry. Schulze wrote up his observations in an academic paper published in 1727 and his ideas became known to the scientific world, but he did not link his experiments to the concept of photography.

Thomas Wedgwood (1771–1805)

Other scientists were carrying out their own experiments, and at the end of the eighteenth century attempts were made to use the effect of light on silver salts to capture the images from the camera obscura.

In England, at the very beginning of the nineteenth century, two enthusiastic young amateur scientists and good friends, Thomas Wedgwood and Humphry Davy, made the connection. Both men came from privileged backgrounds (though Davy less so) and used their financial independence to explore the arts and sciences. Thomas Wedgwood was the

Sir Humphry Davy (1778–1829)

son of Josiah Wedgwood, founder of the famous pottery firm, and (Sir) Humphry Davy became one of the country's leading scientists in the field of chemistry and went on to invent the Davy lamp in 1815 which enabled miners to work safely in the presence of flammable gases. He also recognised the properties of nitrous oxide – laughing gas – which became vital in early medical anaesthesia, and was a pioneer of electrolysis, a process that enabled him to isolate new chemical elements such as sodium, potassium, magnesium and barium.

Wedgwood and Davy experimented with coating paper, and sometimes sheets of white leather, with either silver nitrate or silver chloride. They then laid leaves, insect wings and sheets of glass painted with pictures onto the sensitised surface and exposed them to light, thus producing a silhouette print of the object. Exposure times were long, and the light-sensitive printed image was not 'fixed' as they had no way of neutralising the light sensitivity – further exposure to light resulted in the whole surface of the print eventually going black. They experimented with putting sensitised paper into a camera obscura but found that the light was too weak to affect the paper. Because the prints were not permanent they had to be stored away from daylight in drawers and could only be viewed in a darkened room for a few minutes by the light of a candle. To invited guests, these glimpsed images must have seemed quite magical. Sadly, Wedgwood died only a few years after an account of these discoveries, with a commentary by Davy, was published in 1802. Thus their experiments ceased – Davy's interest waned and he diverted into other research.

In France, similar experiments had been undertaken by Joseph Nicéphore Niépce and his brother, who were both amateur scientists and inventors. By 1813, Niépce had taken early retirement from the army due to ill health and settled on his country estate where he returned to his earlier interest in photochemical images to help him with his work as an amateur artist. Niépce lacked artistic ability; aware of this, he turned to the camera obscura and set about trying to make a permanent record of the images he captured. He experimented with silver chloride on paper and tried fixing the image with nitric acid but became frustrated with the excessively long exposure times and the failures he experienced. He then explored the possibility of using other light-sensitive materials, among them bitumen of Judea, which hardens rather than darkens with exposure to light. As an aspiring artist, Niépce had an interest in etching and the new printing process of lithography, so he applied his methods to metal plates and lithographic stones to make printable images.

He oiled and waxed the print of a traditional etching he owned which made the paper translucent; he then coated a metal plate with bitumen, placed the print on top and in close contact and finally exposed it to strong sunlight. The bitumen protected from the light by the black lines of the image stayed soluble; after washing, these lines appeared as the bare metal of

Joseph Nicéphore Niépce (1765–1833)

the plate, whereas the bitumen in areas that had been exposed to the light hardened and remained.

Niépce then treated the resulting plate as usual for an etching: he immersed it in acid which bit only the bare metal lines of the image while the bitumen acted as a resist to the acid. This created an intaglio printing plate that could be printed in the traditional way. Niépce called his process 'heliography', from the Greek *helios* meaning 'sun'.

In 1826 he made the first successful permanent image using the action of light. The process was somewhat different from previous attempts as it involved coating a sheet of pewter with bitumen and inserting the plate into the back of a camera obscura especially adapted for the purpose. He placed the camera in the window of his workroom with a view over the courtyard of his house. The image was exposed in the camera for eight hours and then the areas of bitumen that had not been hardened by light and remained soluble were washed away with a mixture of oil of lavender and turpentine. The image was positive, with light areas still covered by bitumen and dark areas showing the bare and darkened pewter. The image showed a pigeon house on the left, the top branches of a pear tree appearing above the sloping roof of a barn in the centre and a wing of the house on the right. To the modern viewer this first 'photograph' is very crude and unimpressive – rather disappointing considering its significance.

This image, however, was a one-off. Niépce had intended to create a printable surface by etching the plate and then duplicate the image. However, pewter proved to be too soft as a metal for printing. Niépce turned to silver-plated sheets of copper instead and improved the tonal contrast of his images by blackening the exposed parts of the plate with iodine vapour. It was this refinement of his process that attracted the attention of an ambitious, flamboyant entrepreneur, the Frenchman Jacques Mandé Daguerre.

Daguerre had already made his name in France as a showman and, together with his collaborator Charles Marie Bouton, as the inventor of the Diorama. A spectacular theatrical experience, the Diorama became a hugely popular entertainment in the first half of the nineteenth century. It was an extension of the Panorama, which had been established as an attraction in the previous century: an audience would be ushered into a gallery to view gigantic paintings of panoramic views of cities, land and sea battles, the facades of soaring cathedrals and many other wonders. The paintings could be a hundred metres long and some ran around circular galleries so that the scenes surrounded the public – cries and gasps of astonishment would go up as the views were revealed. The images were painted on layers of transparent fabric, creating a three-dimensional effect and an illusion of reality. These spectacles had become very fashionable, but Daguerre realised that they were limited by being static – no trees or flags were ruffled by the wind, people and vehicles were frozen in time. By the clever use of light, Daguerre added a sense of movement and thus created the Diorama. He painted scenes in different ways on the back and the front of the fabric and manipulated the sources of light – skylights and windows – using blinds and coloured filters made of sheets of fine silks so that the giant screens were lit from the front or from behind. This created dazzling effects as scenes transformed from daytime to night, from summer to winter in a magical way. Real objects used as moving theatrical props also added to the illusion.

Daguerre opened the first Diorama in Paris in 1822 and another in Regent's Park in London the following year. The public were captivated by the show: audiences flocked to see the spectacle and Daguerre basked in public acclaim. He had become a master in his use of light.

Daguerre had begun his career as a painter of scenery for the Panorama and later entered the theatre as a stage designer specialising in creating special effects. The camera obscura was an invaluable tool for such work, providing accuracy and perspective, and Daguerre made full use of it. Aware of the ephemeral nature of his creations, he had also been seeking a way to make a permanent record of his scenes using the camera obscura. He was impressed by Niépce's work and saw the commercial potential of his discoveries, so he persuaded Niépce to join him in a partnership and they signed an agreement in 1829.

In 1827, on a visit to London to see his ailing brother who now lived in England, Niépce was encouraged to publish his experiments but decided to hold back until he had explored the possibilities of exploiting his process for financial gain – he desperately needed to restore the family fortunes, which had declined. With Daguerre's skills as an entrepreneur and showman, Niépce stood a greater chance of benefitting from his process; but fate is cruel. Having passed on all his secrets to Daguerre, Niépce died in 1835. Daguerre continued to work on refining the process and made a breakthrough only two years later. (The outline of the chemistry of the process in the following paragraph can be skipped if you prefer to get on with the story).

Knowing that Niépce had fumed his silvered plates to increase contrast, Daguerre discovered that silver iodide is sensitive to light. He then realised that a latent image was created on the exposed sensitised plate that could be developed and brought out by exposure to mercury vapour. His final triumph came in 1837 when he discovered a way to stop the action of the light and fix the images permanently by washing the exposed plate in a hot solution of saturated salt water. He also managed to reduce the exposure time from nearly eight hours to twenty minutes. Justifiably, Daguerre felt that this was his invention. Although he acknowledged the foundation work of Niépce, he dropped the term heliography and named the process after himself – Daguerreotype.

Niépce's son carried on in partnership with Daguerre and together they tried to sell the rights to the process by public subscription. When this failed, they turned to a distinguished member of the scientific establishment in France, François Arago, for support. Arago was the director of the Observatoire de Paris, secretary of the Académie des Sciences and member of the Chamber of Deputies in the French Parliament. With Arago's power and influence promoting Daguerre's discoveries,

Louis Jacques Mandé Daguerre (1787–1851)

the French government agreed to purchase the rights to his process and proposed to make it freely available to the world. In return Daguerre received a substantial pension and was awarded the Legion of Honour. Niépce's son received a lesser pension in recognition of his father's contribution. A full description of Daguerre's process was revealed to the scientific establishment in Paris on 19 August 1839. It was greeted with excitement by a large crowd buzzing with anticipation and intrigued by the wonders of this new art. Arago's report on the meeting was published in the same month, and Daguerre was proclaimed the inventor of photography. Knowledge of the process was now freely available, but Daguerre, always the astute businessman, had taken out a patent on his process in England five days before the official announcement in Paris.

Public excitement was so great that 'Daguerreomania' quickly took hold. Numerous cartoons appeared that lampooned the rapturous acclaim, and Daguerre was even immortalized in song: one popular comic song sheet for a ditty entitled 'The Daguerreotype' was published with a cover showing a somewhat portly and crazed Daguerre with a smiling sun tucked under his arm.

Daguerre the showman stole the limelight, but others had been working on their own processes. Hippolyte Bayard, another Frenchman with a wonderful name, had sensitised paper instead of the metal substrate that Daguerre was using and had achieved some success with direct positive prints, creating a unique image. Arago, however, wanted to suppress rival processes and persuaded (or, in effect, bribed) Bayard to delay the publication of his discoveries in order not to detract from Daguerre's announcement in 1839. Bayard was passionate about photography and cared little for publicity and fame, but having been given 600 francs to buy equipment and finance further experiments, he later realised he had been duped. In self-mocking mode, Bayard took a photograph of himself in

Cover of comic song sheet

1840, bare-chested and with his eyes closed, entitled *Portrait of the photographer as a drowned man.*

The Daguerreotype received international acclaim but as a process it had serious drawbacks. Each image was unique, and there was no simple way of making a duplicate. An exquisite object, the metal plate with its delicate and sensitive surface had to be protected and sealed behind glass. Manufacturers quickly produced fancy decorative cases in which to mount the plates – creating desirable *objets d'art* to adorn the mantelpiece – but this was merely turning a failing into a virtue. A more obvious problem was that although the image was amazingly sharp and crystal clear, it had to be angled carefully in the light to catch sight of the positive image rather than see a mirror with a faint negative image. If you ever have the opportunity to handle a Daguerrotype you will appreciate these drawbacks, but also its quality. In the years following its initial success, the Daguerreotype process would prove to be a dead end – its application and use was too limited.

In England another pioneering photographer had chosen a different route, and one that proved to be the real future of photography. William Henry Fox Talbot was shocked by Daguerre's declaration that he was the inventor of photography. Spurred into action, Talbot rushed to make a counter-claim and present his own discoveries.

Talbot was a very different personality to his flamboyant rival Daguerre. He was an intellectual, a member of the privileged classes and related to the aristocracy. He was born in 1800 in the magnificent surroundings of the estate of Lacock Abbey, itself a substantial country house built around the ruins of a thirteenth-century monastery near Chippenham in Wiltshire.

But the young Henry also faced difficulties: his father died when he was only five months old and his mother was left with substantial debts. However, she was a resourceful woman; she moved the family out of the Abbey, leased it out and concentrated on restoring the family fortunes. The family did not return to the Abbey until 1827. In the meantime she remarried and her new husband became a warm and supportive stepfather to Henry. Although he was financially relatively comfortable for the rest of his life, these struggles made Talbot careful with money, constantly concerned to preserve the family fortune and provide employment for his large household.

Talbot was educated at Harrow and then at Trinity College, Cambridge, and became a notable scholar and scientist. His

Lacock Abbey

enquiring mind led him to delve into many diverse subjects in both the arts and the sciences; a true polymath, he studied the classics, philosophy, mathematics, astronomy, archaeology, chemistry and botany. He became an active member of the Royal Society, that august organisation founded in the 1660s to promote science, engineering and medicine. He wrote numerous academic papers, and as early as the 1820s he started work on the effects of light and chemical changes in colour. Despite Talbot's establishment background he was a moderate reformer in his political views and became Liberal Member of Parliament for Chippenham from 1832 to 1835 and High Sheriff of Wiltshire in 1840. He had a rather serious nature and was not given to frivolity; content with his own company and somewhat awkward in formal social situations, he did however have a sense of humour and in familiar surroundings could be relaxed and entertaining. His determination and resolve gave him strength in his research, and he also felt a deep sense of responsibility for running the estate and looking after the concerns of the villagers and estate workers.

Talbot married in the same year that he entered Parliament and he and his bride, Constance, went on a belated honeymoon to Lake Como in Italy in 1833. Inspired by the stunning scenery, Talbot started to sketch the landscape but quickly recognised

William Henry Fox Talbot (1800-1877)

his inadequacies as an artist and resorted to drawing aids –
the camera lucida, a device similar in purpose to the camera
obscura which projected an image through a prism onto a
sheet of paper which could then be traced, and the camera
obscura itself. Later, Talbot wrote down this account of his
artistic struggles:

One of the first days of the month of October 1833, I was
amusing myself on the lovely shores of the Lake Como, in

Italy, taking sketches with Wollaston's Camera Lucida, or rather should I say, attempting to take them: but with the smallest possible amount of success. For when the eye was removed from the prism – in which all looked beautiful – I found that the faithless pencil had only left traces on the paper melancholy to behold.

After various fruitless attempts, I laid aside the instrument and came to the conclusion, that its use required a previous knowledge of drawing, which unfortunately I did not process.

I then thought of trying again a method which I had tried many years before. This method was to take a Camera Obscura, and to throw the image of the objects on a piece of transparent tracing paper laid on a pane of glass in the focus of the instrument. On this paper the objects are distinctly seen, and can be traced on it with a pencil with some degree of accuracy, though not without much time and trouble.

He found this method too had its frustrations – the paper kept moving and he just did not have the patience and skill to draw minute details. But he persisted and found that the process stimulated his imagination:

Such, then, was the method which I proposed to try again, and to endeavour, as before, to trace with my pencil the outlines of the scenery depicted on the paper. And this led me to reflect on the inimitable beauty of the picture of nature's painting which the glass lens of the Camera throws upon the paper in its focus – fairy pictures, creations of a moment, and destined as rapidly to fade away.

It was during these thoughts that the idea occurred to me... how charming it would be if it were possible to cause these natural images to imprint themselves durably, and remain fixed upon the paper!

And why should it not be possible? I asked myself.

A familiar figure in scientific circles, Talbot took a natural interest in the experiments that others had already undertaken and had heard and read the accounts of their processes. When he returned from his continental travels in 1834, he decided to test his own theories and speculations by experimenting with silver nitrate and silver chloride, carrying on where others had left off. He brushed the solutions onto writing paper and exposed the sensitised sheets to strong sunlight. Initially he was disappointed by the results – the effect of the light on the solution was weak and slow. But he then realised that he might have taken the wrong approach:

Instead of taking the chloride already formed, and spreading it upon paper. I then proceeded in the following way. The paper was first washed with a strong solution of salt, and when this was dry, it was washed again with nitrate of silver. Of course, chloride of silver was thus formed in the paper, but the result of this experiment was almost the same as before, the chloride not being apparently rendered more sensitive by being formed in this way.

It occurred to him that perhaps he had got the proportions wrong and used too much salt:

A sheet of paper was moistened with a much weaker solution of salt than usual, and when dry, it was washed with nitrate of silver. This paper, when exposed to the sunshine, immediately manifested a far greater degree of sensitiveness than I had witnessed before, the whole of its surface turning black uniformly and rapidly: establishing at once and beyond all question the important fact, that the lesser quantity of salt produced greater effect. And as this circumstance was unexpected, it afforded a simple explanation of the cause why previous inquirers had missed this important result, in their experiments on chloride of silver, namely, because they had always operated with wrong proportions of salt and silver, using plenty of salt in order to produce a perfect chloride,

Contact print or photographic drawing

whereas what was required (it was now manifest) was, to have
a deficiency of salt, in order to produce an imperfect chloride,
or (perhaps it should be called) a subchloride of silver.
With these refinements Talbot was able to produce a series of
beautiful, delicate images:

> ... no difficulty was found in obtaining distinct and very
> pleasing images of such things as leaves, lace, and other flat
> objects of complicated forms and outlines, by exposing them
> to the light of the sun.
>
> The [sensitised] paper being well dried, the leaves, etc. were
> spread upon it, and covered with a glass pressed down tightly,
> and then placed in the sunshine; and when the paper grew
> dark, the whole was carried into the shade, and the objects
> being removed from off the paper, were found to have left
> their images very perfectly and beautifully impressed or
> delineated upon it.

In effect Talbot was making what we would now call 'contact'
prints with real objects. He was able to adequately 'fix' the
images by submersing the exposed paper in a bath of strong salt
water that 'prevented the further action of light upon sensitive
paper'. The images were often exquisite and he would later
give them the name 'photogenic drawings'. In a rather poetic

sense, the name refers to his own attempts at drawing, but with the human hand replaced by rays of light – he saw them literally as 'sun pictures'.

However, when Talbot placed treated sheets of paper in the camera obscura, he found that the sensitivity was not sufficient to create a clear image even after exposure for several hours. The strong light of the sky contrasted well enough with the rooftops of buildings and outlines of trees, but any detail was lost.

By 1835, Talbot had developed more sensitive paper. He discovered that by 'giving it repeated alternate washes of salt and silver, and using it in a moist state, I succeeded in reducing the time necessary for obtaining an image with the Camera Obscura on a bright day to ten minutes.'

That summer Talbot had a number of cameras made. They were tiny – wooden boxes of six centimetres (2 ½ inches) square, with a lens. Talbot had designed these minuscule cameras to shorten the focal length and intensify the concentration of light passing through the lens. The cameras were placed in all corners of the house at Lacock in order to try different views and conditions. His long-suffering wife kept tripping over them; she christened them 'mousetraps' and the name stuck.

'Mousetrap' camera

The results were promising but the images produced in these cameras were tiny – between 25 and 40 mm (1 and 1 ½ inches) square. However, while experimenting in this way it occurred to Talbot that if the paper used to make a photogenic drawing could be made translucent by a relatively simple process of waxing, this negative image could be placed on top of and in contact with another sheet of sensitised paper, weighted down with glass and exposed to daylight to develop a positive image on the second sheet. Talbot had invented the negative – the concept that remained central to the process of modern photography until the introduction of digital photography at the end of the twentieth century.

From a negative it was possible to print many identical positive copies of the image. The oldest surviving paper negative was made by Talbot in August 1835 and has become famous throughout the world, despite its unimpressive subject matter and diminutive size of approximately 25 mm (one inch) square. This small print shows the mullioned oriel window of the library at Lacock Abbey. The window had latticed, diamond-shaped leaded panes of glass and Talbot noted that 'When first made, the squares of glass about 200 in number could be counted with help of a lens'. After waxing the scrap

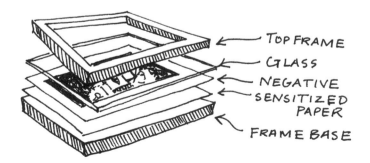

The Oriel window

of paper with the negative image, a positive image of the window was made. How strange that such a tiny object should mark the beginning of a huge change in how people were able to depict the world around them.

As a scientist with a thirst for knowledge it was natural for Talbot, even at this early stage, to find new applications for photography. In the mid-1830s he experimented with taking photographs through the lens of a microscope, capturing the complex structures of cross-sections of botanic specimens and insect wings – a technique that has had a huge significance for our understanding of nature.

Talbot had made great strides with his methods but they still needed considerable improvement, and he was tiring of

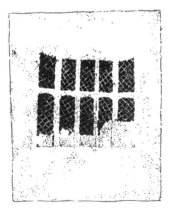

Negative and positive print of the Oriel window

Insect wing – salt paper print, 1839

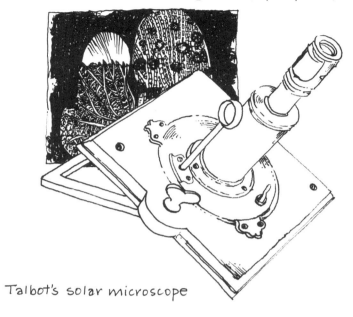

Talbot's solar microscope

the subject. For the next few years his attention was distracted away from photography by the many other studies and projects he pursued. But when he heard of the announcement of Daguerre's invention in January 1839, he was provoked into action.

In an effort to establish a prior claim to the discovery of photography, Talbot called on the aid of his fellow scientist, the influential and distinguished Michael Faraday, who quickly arranged an exhibition of examples of Talbot's photogenic drawings at the Royal Institution in London, on 25 January 1839. A few days later, on the last day of the month, Talbot presented a paper entitled 'Some Account of the Art of Photogenic Drawing' to the Royal Society, and in February he presented a second, more detailed description of his process which was published.

There was a strong rivalry between Daguerre and Talbot: Talbot even wrote to Daguerre's colleagues to assert that he was the inventor of photography. In these early days, Talbot came off worse. People who had travelled to Paris to see Daguerreotypes came back with enthusiastic reports of the brilliance and sharpness of Daguerre's images, which were also larger than those that Talbot was able to produce. In their decorative cases, on shiny silver plates, they were precious and jewel-like. Talbot's images, in comparison, seemed dull and discoloured (they often had a bluish or sepia tone). Furthermore, the images seemed rather soft and lacking sharpness of focus, owing to the fibrous, matt quality of the writing paper used as the substrate and, indeed, for the negative – the light had to pass through the thickness of the paper which created an even softer appearance. Exposure times were still far too long – as much as two hours – as the paper was still not sensitive enough. This restricted the subject matter and made portraiture impossible. No wonder the public flocked to get their portraits taken by the Daguerreotype process, leaving Talbot's work to be appreciated by the few who had the vision to realise the significance of the negative/positive process and the paper print. Realising that his process was far from perfect, Talbot was spurred into undertaking more research.

At times he benefitted from other people's discoveries. John Herschel – son of the great astronomer William Herschel and a family friend of the Talbots – and another distinguished scientist, the Rev. J. B. Reade, had independently been experimenting with photography; they both had recognised that gallic acid accelerated the process by increasing sensitivity. Herschel mentioned this to Talbot who had already read about it in a paper by Reade.

A breakthrough came in September 1840, when Talbot discovered that he could produce a 'latent' image on the paper in a fraction of the previous exposure time which could then

Sir John Herschel (1792–1871)

be developed as a second stage of the process. But what is a 'latent' image? In simple terms, the paper is sensitised and exposed but the image remains invisible to the eye until further chemicals are applied, the paper is warmed and the image 'magically' appears and gradually darkens until fully developed. The image must then be fixed.

Readers with a more general interest may wish to skip what follows, but for those who revel in the scientific facts, here is a brief but detailed description of Talbot's improved process, quoted from *A Concise History of Photography* by Helmut and Alison Gernsheim (Thames and Hudson, 1965):

Good quality writing paper was coated successively with solutions of silver nitrate and potassium iodide, forming silver iodide, then further sensitised with solutions of gallic acid and silver nitrate. After exposure the latent image was developed with a further application of gallo-nitrate of silver solution – which had the same function as the mercury developer in the daguerreotype – and the picture became visible when the paper was warmed by the fire for one or two minutes. The negative was fixed with potassium bromide (later hyposulphite of soda) and then rinsed with water. The positive print was made on Photogenic Drawing paper (not developed).

Herschel, who made many contributions to the development of photography and even held back from publishing his experiments so as not to distract from his friend Talbot's announcement, had also recommended the use of hyposulphite of soda (later known as 'hypo') for fixing the image.

Talbot felt he had at last fully resolved the problems of sensitivity and fixing the image and developed a viable process for photography on paper. He had also managed to reduce the time it took to take a photograph to speeds that came close to the Daguerreotype. Now his first instinct was to protect his discovery by applying for a patent in 1841. He gave his process the name 'calotype', derived from the Greek *kalos* meaning 'beautiful', but it also became known as 'Talbotype'. Under the patent, Talbot was able to issue licences to others who wanted to use the process for commercial purposes.

Talbot wrote to Herschel on 17 Marsch 1841:

I have taken a patent for the calotype, but nevertheless intend that use of it shall be entirely free to the scientific world. … There appears to me to be no end to the prospect of scientific research which photography has opened.

Herschel replied:

You are quite right in patentizing the Calotype. With the liberal interpretation you propose in exercising the patent right, no one can complain. And I must say, I never heard of a more promising subject for a *lucrative* patent of which I heartily give you joy…

However, it could be argued that Talbot's rather obsessive need to tie up his discoveries with patents (he took out further patents on photography in 1843, 1849 and 1851) only restricted the take-up of his process and led to litigation. No doubt some of his wealthy scientific colleagues amongst the upper classes frowned upon this rather commercial approach. However, Talbot lacked entrepreneurial drive and never really dedicated himself to promoting his process or selling licences; throughout the 1840s he was distracted by many areas of research unrelated to photography.

A miniature portrait painter, Henry Collen, became the first licensee under the patent and set up a calotype studio in London in August 1841. When his licence lapsed in 1844 it was taken up by Talbot's friend and distinguished fellow scientist and Daguerreotypist, Antoine Claudet. Talbot's patent did not apply to Scotland so David Octavius Hill and Robert Adamson did not need a licence to set up the only calotype studio north of the border and produce some wonderful images. But generally the process was slow to be adopted. Talbot needed a more practical way to demonstrate the advantages of his methods, and what better way than to set up a commercial photographic studio to mass-produce calotypes?

This brief foray into the history of photography shows that it is difficult to attribute the invention of the process to one particular person or a particular date – the truth is that it was the culmination of various discoveries over a period of centuries and the contributions of a number of scholars and enthusiastic amateur scientists.

Now let us return to the story of the Reading Establishment and follow Talbot on an imaginary journey he might well have made to visit this new venture.

Photography comes to Reading

Picture an early summer morning in 1844. Talbot has arranged to visit the Reading establishment on his way to London to stay overnight at his club and attend a lecture at the Royal Society. He has instructed the stables to have the carriage ready at 8.30am in order to give him plenty of time to catch the 9.40 'Up' train to Reading. The road from Lacock to his nearest station at Chippenham is rather rough and ready and although it is only about three miles, he wants to leave in time to allow for possible delays – an unpredictable blockage by a farm cart or a herd of cattle.

Leaving the warmth of his study, Talbot enters the vast draughty hall of the Abbey. The stone floor is dappled with spots of bright colour from the sun passing through the medieval stained glass of the rose window. Here, waiting by the great arch over the main door, his butler stands ready with his overcoat, top hat and portmanteau. The hall is a cavernous room, ancient in atmosphere but in fact remodelled in a high Gothic revival style in the 1750s by one of Talbot's ancestors. The barrelled ceiling above is studded with coats of arms and the walls are dotted with ecclesiastical niches containing the figures of saints and some bizarre and macabre terracotta sculptures.

Talbot's carriage awaits

The morning light floods in as the great doors are opened and Talbot steps out into the chilly air, pausing to take in the view. He descends one of the double flights of stone steps to the forecourt below, turns right and makes his way, shoes crunching on the gravel path, to the high gothic arch at the entrance to the old Tudor stable yard. He pulls a gold watch from his waistcoat pocket and checks the time.

Talbot is followed by the butler, who hands the portmanteau to the driver and opens the carriage door. The horses snort and their breath freezes in the chill of the morning. A crack from the whip, and they clatter down the drive and out onto the road. The carriage passes a group of farm workers from the village and they doff their hats as Talbot wishes them a good morning.

The journey to the station is bracing, but Talbot arrives in the market town of Chippenham in good time. Approaching the station, Talbot sees in front of him the massive brick arches of the new bridge carrying the railway line. The carriage turns right; the horses strain as they climb the steep hill to the station and finally pull up at the entrance. The station has only been open for three years. Positioned north of the market and the High Street, the building is in the Italianate style, a single-story villa constructed in Bath stone. A low-pitched roof, topped by tall decorative chimneys, extends beyond the walls to form a canopy on all four sides of the building. This rather elegant design, although modest in scale,

is the work of Isambard Kingdom Brunel, who brought the railway to Chippenham in 1841 as part of the construction of the Great Western Railway and used a room there as a drawing office.

The train pulls into the station on time and Talbot climbs into one of the first class carriages. The design of the carriages resembles a number of stage coaches joined together on a single frame. Talbot settles down in the plush and comfortable upholstered surroundings and pulls the blind down to cut off the glare of the morning sun. He can now relax and enjoy the copy of *The Times* he purchased at the bookshop on the station. The station master shouts at two scruffy workers to get a move on, pushing them into the third class wagons, which are little more than open cattle trucks with bench seats – the poorer classes have to endure the smoke and cinders while huddled together to keep warm. The whistle blows at precisely 9.40am and the slow puffing of the engine begins, building to a steady rhythm as the train gathers speed.

The next stop is Wootton Bassett, then Swindon Junction, Shrivenham, Faringdon Road and on to Steventon, Goring and Pangbourne; the train is finally due to arrive at Reading at 11.50am. Deep in thought, Talbot scribbles ideas in his notebook, occasionally glancing up to enjoy the passing views. As the train passes Basildon Park his attention is taken by a Thames barge boat, low in the water from its heavy load, slowly ploughing its way up the river pulled by a steaming giant of a horse;

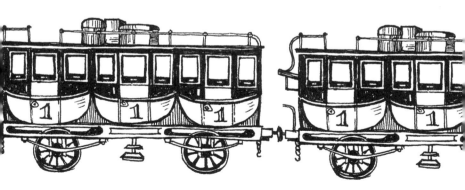

and he considers how this new technology of the railway is ruining the future for the canals. Approaching Reading, Talbot looks to his left and admires the river and the meadows beyond where cattle are grazing, and the view across to the village of Caversham. His view to the right is of the rapidly expanding and bustling town of Reading. Talbot again consults his pocket watch dangling from its gold chain: the train is exactly on time.

The station at Reading has also been designed by Brunel but lacks the refinement of Chippenham. Brunel had originally planned 'an extravaganza' for Reading but his designs were rejected as too expensive. Annoyed and disappointed, Brunel went to the other extreme and built two stations on the south (town) side of the tracks, both rather basic and uninspired – one block for the Down line and one for the Up line. This is already proving to be a strange and inefficient arrangement because the trains have to depart from the main line on loops to each platform. The idea is to save passengers having to cross over the main line on a bridge (as is the usual arrangement with platforms on either side of the track). But the result is that trains have to cross over the lines, which causes delays and the potential for collision if the signalman is distracted. What is more, the brakes are not always reliable.

There is a clattering of doors as passengers alight onto the platform of the Up station. Talbot steps down from his carriage and looks around for a porter to take his portmanteau into storage for the day until his return for the onward journey to Paddington. The platform is covered by a zinc roof with a central skylight and supported on cast iron pillars – in the enclosed space the noise is tremendous. The engine is hissing, station officials are shouting and whistling, doors are banging; the waiting passengers, anxious to board, are in danger of tripping over the trunks and luggage left in piles on the platform.

Once out on the forecourt of the station, Talbot ignores the cab drivers shouting for trade and decides to walk. The weather is clement and Henneman, at the studio in Russell Terrace, is only about a twenty-five minutes walk away, so the prospect of a stroll is inviting. The land in front of the station is a broad open space clear of buildings, and a wide, straight approach road leads to the junction with Friar Street, one of the town's main thoroughfares. Either side of the road are deep ditches where the soil has been excavated to build up the embankment and level the track. Talbot strides out, passing the Great Western Hotel standing in isolation; it is in the last stages of construction and due to open very soon. A large, solid classical building inspired by Brunel, it is the first purpose-built railway hotel in the country. The proprietors of the numerous coaching inns in the town are loud in their opposition to the development – the coming of the railway has already resulted in the closure of many coaching services, which have been so much a part of Reading's prosperity, and this hotel is the final straw – they fear for the future of their businesses.

At the junction with Friar Street Talbot passes through the grand gateway that marks the entrance to the station approach. He turns right and crosses the dusty road to the far side. As he does so a small scruffy boy tips his cap and rushes before him to scoop up the steaming deposit left by a passing horse and shovel it into a sack. Were Talbot to turn left into Friar Street it would lead him to the ancient church of St Laurence and the Town Hall, behind which lies the site of the demolished Reading Abbey with its few remaining ruins. At the other end of the street is the Bridewell of Greyfriars, originally a fourteenth-century church built by Franciscan friars but now a miserable gaol or 'house of correction', little used and in a dilapidated state. In the *Berkshire Post Office Directory*, published by John Snare, a local printer in Minster Street, which Talbot consulted when looking for premises in Reading, Friar Street is described as a 'fine and spacious thoroughfare'. However, it is punctuated by dark alleyways leading off to cramped and dingy courtyards – evidence of the medieval origins and layout of the town. Nevertheless it is a respectable street and full of bustling shops and traders. Talbot wanders past a number of shoemakers, tailors and beer houses; past the dressmakers run by the Misses Poulton – the shop window displays the latest fashions from London and a dazzling display of silks and ribbons. Looking down Friar's Court, he pauses to look at the carved ivory handles of the walking sticks in the window

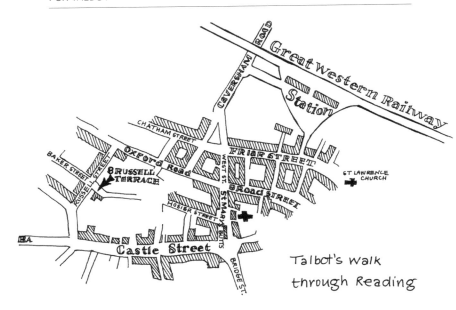

Talbot's walk
through Reading

of Joseph Beard, the umbrella maker; passing Union Street he sees the cascading array of baskets strung up from the façade of William Davie's shop; then the grander premises of Thomas Lovegrove, solicitor, whose name is engraved on a polished brass plate beside the door, and the more humble establishment of Sarah, the straw bonnet maker. At the end of the street are the Bridewell and the forlorn buildings of St Laurence's workhouse.

Now Talbot takes a left turn into West Street and walks past a greengrocer's whose boxes and sacks full of fresh vegetables spill out onto the street; he ducks to avoid the carcases of rabbits and pheasants dangling above his head outside a butcher's. A big woman with ruddy complexion and swollen red hands pushes in front of Talbot balancing a big basket of dirty clothes on her hip and nearly knocks him over; she barges through the door of a laundry which opens into a steamy interior festooned with lines and wet sheets and swears at a ragged little girl struggling with a heavy pail as soapy, scalding, dirty water slops onto the brick floor. Next door is Henry Fellows, tinman, and further down the more genteel premises of a china dealer and a furrier; next to them is the Mitre Tavern and chop house.

Crossing over the entrance to Broad Street, the main street of the town, the road in front broadens out into a market place called St Mary's Butts, a name given in medieval times as it was a place for archery practice. Many of the cottages – timber-framed with walls of wattle-and-daub and upper floors jutting out over the pavement – are very old and run down, some even squalid. Further down Talbot passes some larger businesses, including Heelas & Sons Wool Warehouse, and some less salubrious establishments such as Mrs Gulle, slopseller, and plenty of inns, beerhouses and a pawnbroker. About halfway down, Talbot glances up to the left at the clock on the chequered flint tower of St Mary's Church rising up above a row of almshouses that line the road; a gap between the houses leads to the church. Here the road becomes so wide that a row of terraced buildings has been erected on an island in the middle of the road. The end gable of the first shop facing Talbot is smothered by posters pasted on haphazardly and now peeling and flapping in the breeze. Large decorative letters printed from woodblocks announce a variety of events and extol the miraculous benefits of amazing products. Talbot has to be careful here as the street is full of horse-drawn vehicles of all sorts. He picks his way through the traffic to cross the expanse of dirt road.

Talbot tries to keep to the pavement but is often forced to step into the gutter to skirt around the voluminously hooped dresses of the ladies. He takes the fork in the road to the right of the island of shops and then turns right into Castle Street, walking past the magnificent columns of the classical portico of St Mary's Episcopal Chapel that has recently been added to the façade. Next to the Chapel is the Sun Inn, the oldest coaching inn in the town. As well as the usual trades and retailers, the properties in Castle Street – progressing in size and status as the road goes up the hill – include the houses of gentlemen and professionals: a surgeon, a miniature artist, a Major General and academic establishments, among them Miss Webb's Ladies Seminary and Mr Richards' Oxford House Classical Academy. Members of the Jesse family still live in Castle Hill House, in the shadow of the ancient cedar tree whose canopy towers above the rooftops. The road climbs and at the top runs into a junction with the Bath Road ahead and Coley Avenue

8 Russell Terrace

on the left. Talbot takes the turning on the right which bears round into a residential road called Russell Street. Comfortable middle-class family homes line the left-hand side of the street; in the distance where the road ends, Talbot can see the façade of Holy Trinity Church in the Oxford Road. The right-hand side of the street is open ground – plots of land waiting for the developers. Halfway down Russell Street is a crossroads with Baker Street to the left and Russell Terrace to the right.

Turning into Russell Terrace, Talbot has reached his destination: ahead of him on the right stands a row of terraced properties, and the first building is number 8 – the Reading photographic studio. Talbot knows that Henneman is probably at work in the darkroom at the rear of the building so instead of knocking at the front door, he takes the path down the side of the house and garden until he reaches an iron gate in the wall. Peering over, he can see a framework of wooden racking almost filled with frames containing negatives and sensitised paper being exposed in the strong sun. Henneman emerges from the door of a conservatory built on the rear of the building carrying another frame; he is without his jacket and his sleeves are rolled up. In his early thirties, Henneman is average in stature, a trim figure with a refined face, dark mutton chop side whiskers and a thick mop of wavy hair swept to one side of his parting. He raises his hand to shade his eyes, immediately recognises Talbot at the gate and shouts out a greeting in his strong Dutch accent. The two men obviously know each other well, but how is it that Talbot has put so much trust and investment in setting Henneman up in this business?

John Henderson, in his reminiscences of 1898, recalled his friendship with Henneman and affectionately described him as 'nothing like the typical Dutchman, but a lively, volatile fellow who had lived much in Paris, & become more of a Frenchman'. We shall return to Henderson and his involvement in the Establishment later but for now let us concentrate on Henneman and his role and relationship with Talbot.

Nicolaas Henneman was born in 1813 and brought up in the small agricultural community of Heemskerk in northern Holland. As a youth of seventeen he entered service, joining the household of the Dutch Minister of Foreign Affairs to the Portuguese Court. He remained on the staff even after the death of the Minister, moving to Paris to continue in service with his widow. Life in the French capital opened up many opportunities for Henneman, who flourished in the cultured atmosphere of the city, learning a number of languages and growing in confidence and experience.

In 1838, when he was in his mid-twenties, he came to England and took up employment in the Talbot household as courier to Lady Elizabeth, Talbot's mother. Soon after, he became personal valet to Talbot himself and, despite being a servant, quickly gained Talbot's respect and friendship. Henneman was therefore working closely with Talbot just at the time when the latter was making such strides in his photographic experiments, and he supported him during the stressful period around the announcement of his discoveries to the Royal Society. Known for his easy manner and sense of humour, Henneman was also held in affection by other members of the family. Given his obvious intelligence and enquiring mind it is not surprising that Henneman became caught up in his master's experiments and went on to become a valued assistant central to Talbot's activities. He accompanied Talbot on trips to France where Talbot photographed great cathedrals and, closer to home, the two men made a series of studies of the

Henneman taking a photograph

architecture of Oxford. Henneman himself also became the subject of Talbot's photographs: he was frequently called upon to model: playing chess, sawing wood and many other poses.

Henneman took to photography, so when Talbot decided to set up a photographic studio it would have been natural to turn to Henneman to run it. Records show that by March 1843, Talbot had ceased paying Henneman as a valet but was financing him to find premises, start equipping the studio and darkroom and buy in materials. It would seem that they were now in a form of partnership, with Talbot providing the money and Henneman doing the work.

So why did Talbot and Henneman choose Reading as the location for a photographic establishment? Most likely the costs of renting property were lower in the provinces than in London – and this was a financially risky enterprise. Talbot had been negotiating over selling exclusive rights to photographers in London to produce calotypes, thus making it impossible for him to do so himself. Another important factor was the weather and the quality of the air. The notorious smogs and pollution from the belching chimneys of London limited the days of strong sunlight that was so necessary for the printing of the photographs, and the air in Reading at the time was relatively clear and unpolluted. On a practical level, Reading was conveniently located, being geographically roughly halfway between Lacock and Paddington, the London terminus for the Great Western Railway. Travelling by train was the quickest, most comfortable and reliable form of transport for Talbot, and also for Henneman's visits to Lacock.

Reading Station opened in March 1840 to great excitement and ceremony. Isambard Kingdom Brunel and the Great Western company directors travelled down the line from London on a trial journey and were greeted by cheering crowds. By the end of the month the railway was open to the public and again crowds gathered either side of the track to watch the coming and going of the locomotives, fascinated by the spectacle of these huffing and puffing steaming monsters but also astonished at their speed – just one hour and five minutes from Paddington to Reading.

Talbot was an enthusiastic supporter of the railways. He had made his first journey in 1831 on the new Liverpool–Manchester line. His cousin, Kit Talbot, was a close associate of Brunel, and in 1853 he wrote to Talbot about the problem with the crossing lines at the Reading stations:

> Did you but know how your life depends on the steadiness of the signalmen at the parts where other railways meet and cross! I said one day to Brunel while we were coming up [to London] 'I am always glad when we have passed the Reading points, they are so complicated… ' I wanted his assurance there was no danger but his reply was 'And so am I'.

The railway line all the way to Bristol had been completed

and opened in 1841 and had already had an effect on the expansion and prosperity of Reading. The iron foundry in Katesgrove Lane had supplied materials for the line and would later develop into the Reading Iron Works, employing at one point 360 workers. The coming of the railway facilitated the rapid expansion of a number of businesses: the biscuit manufacturers Huntley & Palmers (Thomas Huntley had formed a partnership with George Palmer in 1841) and the corn and seed merchants Sutton Seeds in particular would become two of the major employers in the town, establishing 'global brands' and exporting to the world.

The population of Reading was approaching 20,000 in the early 1840s. Improvements were being made to street lighting and paving and, although there were serious problems with the supply of clean water, conditions generally were getting better for the citizens of the town. It was not just the

SUTTON & SONS
Reading

HUNTLEY & PALMERS SUPERIOR FANCY SWEET BISCUITS READING

commercial side of Reading that was thriving. There was a lively, stimulating and cultured community growing up in the town, eager to explore the arts and sciences. In 1841, the Reading Pathological Society was formed by the staff of the Royal Berkshire Hospital, a magnificent stone building opened in 1839 that did a great deal to improve public health. The aims of the Society were to 'promote the advancement of knowledge and interest in the art and science of medicine'. A Philosophical Institute had been established for some years, an Athenaeum was founded in 1842, and in the same year the famous local author Mary Russell Mitford laid the foundation stone for a new Mechanics' Institution. This grand, impressive classical building with its pediment and sturdy columns – now the Great Expectations Hotel – was built in London Street next door to the premises of George Lovejoy's Southern Counties Library, the largest subscription library in the south of England. Lovejoy was a man of liberal views and considerable intellect; he was also a jovial character and hospitable in nature, and the library, which included a bookshop and stationery department, had become a regular meeting place for those of an inquiring mind – many great literary figures and men of science dropped in for a chat at Lovejoy's. Charles Dickens, William Makepeace Thackeray, Wilkie Collins, Charles Reade, Thomas Noon Talfourd, Charles Kingsley, Algernon Swinburne, Mary Russell Mitford and John Walter, the owner of *The Times* newspaper, were amongst Lovejoy's friends and acquaintances.

So Reading had many advantages for Talbot and Henneman: an expanding commercial environment, good communications and a stimulating and receptive social community of the intelligentsia.

Number 8 Russell Terrace was at the end of a row of substantial terraced houses. The original building had been enlarged and extended at the rear to accommodate a small

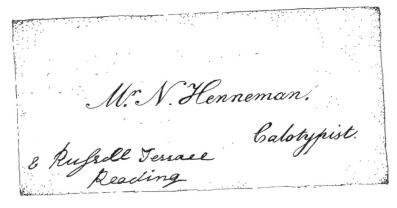

Henneman's trade card

private school for young children named the Diocesan School, which was run by a Mr Charles Brown. It had closed down not long before Henneman and Talbot took over the lease and was now only occupied by an old housekeeper. It was suited to their purpose as on the ground floor at the back of the building was a windowless room that provided a darkroom, and behind this was a conservatory which made a sunlit studio that opened out through double doors onto a yard that had been used as a playground.

Henneman moved to Reading sometime around the end of 1843 and the beginning of 1844. By March 1844 he had become sufficiently established in the town to come to the notice of the local press. The *Reading Mercury* published a short article mentioning him on 2 March:

There is now a gentleman in this town (Mr. N. Henneman, Russell Terrace), who has for sometime been engaged with Mr. F. Talbot (the inventor) in carrying out experiments and effecting improvements in this beautiful art [of photography]. The lovers of science would be highly gratified at witnessing the interesting process, as it is skilfully conducted by this gentleman, and we have heard with pleasure that it is not improbable that a lecture will be given upon this subject at the New Rooms [as the Mechanics' Institution was known] by him. It is a subject quite new in the circle of the arts, and one which possesses unusual interest.

(The lecture anticipated in this article was in fact not delivered by Henneman for another year.)

Another reason that might have made Reading a suitable location for the Establishment was the lack of rival photographic businesses – Daguerreotype studios were rapidly opening up elsewhere but so far had not come to Reading so the way was clear for Henneman and Talbot. However, Talbot did encounter a famous Reading citizen who proved to be a rival, and the two men soon engaged in a war of words.

William Havell was a painter of considerable reputation. He was born in Reading in 1782, the son of Luke Havell, a drawing master who had a small shop in London Street selling paintings and providing a glazing service. William had been a pupil at Reading Grammar School, where his father taught, and, having trained as an artist, exhibited regularly at the Royal Academy. He was a founder member of the Society of Painters in Water Colours, a medium in which he excelled. With a growing reputation, Havell embarked on some extraordinary adventures and travels, spending years abroad in China and India, which must have seemed exotic and distant at the beginning of the nineteenth century and involved long, treacherous sea voyages. He then spent time in Italy before returning to England.

Havell had three brothers who all became artists of note. George Havell specialised in painting animals, Edmund Havell succeeded his father as a drawing master in Reading and Frederick James Havell became a printmaker specialising in line engraving and mezzotint. It was with his brother Fredrick that William shared an interest in the new invention of photogenic drawing. They had conducted their own

William Havell (1782–1857)

experiments, focusing on the reproduction of works of art, and had been excited by the hurried paper that Talbot submitted to the Royal Society in January 1839, which outlined his process in answer to Daguerre's announcements.

In his paper, Talbot had revealed his secret of how to fix the image; by adopting this method, William and Frederick were able to complete what they considered to be their own new technique. They claimed that they had developed a process 'for the delineation of work of the artist's pencil' and at the end of March 1839 exhibited specimens at the Royal Society. On 6 April 1839, the journal *The Athenaeum* published a detailed account of the Havells' process in a section entitled 'Our Weekly Gossip':

The interest excited by the new art – Photogenic Drawing – still continues. ... Mr Talbot, in his first Report, ... refers to shadow pictures formed by exposing paintings on glass to solar light. This idea has been carried out by Mr. William Havell, who has in this way produced some admirable etchings, and who last week addressed to us a full explanation of this process, but unfortunately too late for publication in Saturday's paper. 'A square of thin glass,' Mr. Havell observes, 'was placed over the well known etching by Rembrandt of "Faust conjuring Mephistopheles to appear in the form of a bright star." I then painted on the high lights with thick white lead mixed with copal varnish, and sugar of lead to make it dry quickly; for the half tints I made the white less opaque with the varnish, and graduated the tints off into the glass for the deep shadows. I allowed this to dry, and the following day, Feb. 27, retouched the whole, by removing with the point of a knife the white ground, to represent the dark etched lines of the original; the glass thus painted when placed upon black paper looked like a powerful mezzotint engraving. I placed a sheet of prepared paper upon the painted surface, and, to make the contact perfect, put three layers of flannel at the back, and tied the whole down to a board. There happened to be bright sun, and in ten minutes the parts of the glass exposed had made a deep purplish black on the paper. On removing the glass I had a tolerably good impression, but the half tints had absorbed too much of the violet ray. I immediately painted the parts over with black on the other side of the glass, which answers to the practice of engravers in stopping out when a plate is bitten in too fast by acid - this may be wiped off, renewed, or suffered to remain, at pleasure. There is no advantage in letting the glass remain too long in the light, as it deepens the middle tints and does not blacken the shadows in the same proportion. The fixation with salt entirely failed; but with the iodide of potassium succeeded very well...

Havell goes on to describe various subtle ways of improving and 'invigorating' the image by working on the glass; the results created the effect of a 'spirited drawing with pen and ink, or under the hands of the engraver, a highly-finished engraving'. Other refinements produced the effect of lithography or a mezzotint print. At the end of the article is an editorial comment on the rivalry between Talbot's and Daguerre's processes:

> While on this subject, we may observe that some of our contemporaries continue to argue respecting the discoveries of Mr. Fox Talbot and M. Daguerre, as if a doubt yet existed as to priority. There can be no doubt on the subject. Mr. Talbot himself states that for four or five years his attention has been directed to the subject; whereas there is abundant proof that M. Daguerre had made great progress in his discovery – had indeed produced many drawings more than a dozen years since. But we repeat, that the processes are entirely different, and the results different; and having seen specimens of all, including among the best those of Mr. Talbot, Sir John Herschel, and Mr. Havell, we distinctly state that those of M. Daguerre far excel any which have been produced in this country.

In hindsight it seems strange that critics and commentators were bedazzled by the brilliance of Daguerre's images and blind to their limitations, and that they failed to recognise the significance and long-term implications of Talbot's use of the negative.

Talbot, always wary of and sensitive to the perceived rival claims of others, had already published an indignant response to the Havells' process as described in the *Literary Gazette* on 23 March 1839, pointing out that he had already published a description of drawing on glass for such purposes. However, this was rather unfair on William: in the same edition of the journal he noted that their process was in one respect quite the opposite of Talbot's. Their aim was to deliberately delineate the 'work of the artist's pencil' whereas in Talbot's process 'natural objects may be made to delineate themselves <u>without</u> the aid of the artist's pencil'. It seems their claim was not so concerned with who invented photogenic drawing but with the particular application of reproducing an artist's work. Talbot's apparent over-sensitivity might have been caused by his discovery that the Havells had been working with the engraver J. T. Wilmore, who had been looking into taking out a patent on the process. Wilmore wrote a letter to the editor of the *Literary Gazette,* published on 6 April 1839, defending their position:

> The interest which you have taken in the question of priority of invention... induces me to offer to your attention what I certainly claim to have been with me an original invention, whatever unpublished priority may be claimed by Mr. Fox Talbot. I herewith send you two specimens of works which I have executed, without the slightest idea that any one before me had ever thought of the process by which I produced them. If it be a subject of reproach that a man, having made a discovery which he believes to be valuable, attempts to secure a personal benefit by a patent, it will apply to hundreds of inventions for which patents have been obtained. I did, certainly, with two other artists, attempt to secure one.... Self-protection prompted this, – for the new art, as it was spoken of, threatened us with the loss of our occupation [engraving]. ... the charge comes with an ill grace.... Why Mr. Talbot should have felt sore, and jealous of the improvements... I cannot understand... what he did disclose was only an amusement – a plaything. Others, and among them Mr. Havell and myself, have endeavoured to found upon it an art...

The *Literary Gazette* published Talbot's response on 13 April:

> Dear Sir, – I have the greatest dislike to controversy, which I regard as a complete waste of time. I consider it sufficient to have stated, once [and] for all, in your widely circulated

journal, that I discovered the art of obtaining photogenic pictures from glass in the year 1834.... . But since that account [to the Royal Society on 31 January 1839] seemed to have been already in some measure forgotten by the public, I stated it again, and in fuller manner. How could I do otherwise, when I found that a patent had been applied for this identical process?

William Havell also wrote to the editor of the *Literary Gazette* on 13 April, but he was more diplomatic and dignified in his response and anxious to distance himself from Wilmore:

Sir, – My name having been lately frequently published, as seemingly connected with the party who attempted to secure a patent to themselves... I beg to explain, that I knew nothing of their proceedings till after the attempt had been made, and then expressed my decided disapprobation and opposition to the whole affair. The art of etching on glass was practised many years ago, and specimens printed and published by Mr. Blake, the celebrated artist and engraver: 'its application to photography very readily suggested itself'.

But here this lively dispute peters out. Frederick Havell suffered a mental breakdown and died the following year.

Discover Talbot's Reading

The images on the following pages are all views of Reading taken sometime between 1844 and 1846, possibly by Talbot but more likely by Nicolaas Henneman. They are all salt prints taken from calotype negatives.

1. Russell Street
2. Coley Avenue
3. Tudor buildings in Castle Street
4. St Mary's Church
5. The Oracle in Minster Street
6. St Giles' Church
7. London Street
7a Close-up of George Lovejoy's Library
8. St Laurence's church
8a St Laurence's church from the Market Place
9. The Abbey Gateway
10. Villas in Eldon Square
    The Reading Establishment of Russell Street (1.)

1 Russell Street

View of the comfortable terraced houses that lined Russell Street and are still there today. The turning into Russell Terrace is on the right but out of sight. The church seen at the bottom of the street on the Oxford Road is Holy Trinity.

2 Coley Avenue at the top of Castle Hill

3 Tudor buildings in Castle Street

These gabled and timber-framed buildings with their upper stories protruding over the pavement have survived, little changed, and are today occupied by solicitor's offices. The brick building on the right dates from the early eighteenth century.

4 St Mary's Church before restoration in the 1860s
The churchyard is shaded by large trees today and still an attractive
part of the town. The photograph was taken from Minster Street.

5 Entrance to the Oracle in Minster Street
The Oracle was a workhouse for the poor that was built with
funds left in the will of John Kendrick, who died in 1624. It was
demolished in 1850, not long after this photograph was taken. The
site is near to Reading's biggest shopping centre of the same name.
Sections of the massive gates which were hung in the archway have
been restored and are on show in Reading Museum.

6 St Giles' Church, looking down Southampton Street
This early church dates back to the twelfth century and was badly
damaged in a siege of the town during the Civil War in 1643. It was
heavily restored in the 1870s, after this photograph was taken.

7 Looking down London Street
In the centre of the photograph is George Lovejoy's Library and bookshop. These premises have changed little and are now occupied by RISC and the Global Café. To the left is the Mechanics' Institution, which is now the Great Expectations hotel and public house.

7a Close-up of George Lovejoy's Library in London Street
It is possible that some of Talbot's Calotypes are on display.

8 St Laurence's Church

8a St Laurence's Church from the Market Place

The arcade or covered walk seen here which ran along the outer wall was eventually demolished in 1867. Beneath it were the parish stocks, and at the eastern end there was a small 'lock-up' for offenders. The building is still in use today as a mission church for young people.

9 The Abbey Gateway

Overlooking Forbury Gardens, the Abbey gateway is still a familiar landmark in the town. In this photograph, it is in a dilapidated state. The fabric of the building was heavily restored by the eminent architect Giles Gilbert Scott after it collapsed in a storm in 1861.

10 Villas in the corner of Eldon Square
These remain today, little changed.

The Reading Establishment
The view is of the back of the premises in Russell Terrace. This
is a staged photograph probably taken for publicity purposes and
shows various applications of photography. On the left a gentleman
is photographing a portrait, showing that photography can be used
for reproducing works of art. Next to him, a gentleman who might
be Talbot himself is taking a portrait photograph of a seated gentleman whose head is being kept still by a clamp at the back of his head

during the lengthy exposure. To Talbot's right, 'the boy' is checking the frames containing the negatives and the sensitised paper during the printing process. Beside him, Henneman is taking a picture of a copy of Canova's sculpture, *The Three Graces*. The man kneeling down is adjusting a device known as a focometer which was used as a focusing aid. Other individuals are difficult to identify but might include John Henderson, Alfred Harrison and Thomas Malone.

At work in the Establishment

As well as involving Henneman in his experiments at Lacock, Talbot had also made use of other servants, in particular Charles Porter, who undertook most of the routine photographic printing in the darkroom that Talbot had set up in the house. Initially, Henneman worked alone in Reading – his secretive, lonesome activities causing suspicion – but soon he was joined by Porter and another servant from Lacock called Murray. The three of them sensitised the paper, Henneman took the exposures and then they processed the prints together. Henneman was also managing the business. But this arrangement was only temporary – Henneman's assistants were paid by him but they were only 'on loan' for a period while the business was getting established. On their return to Lacock, Henneman needed to recruit some staff.

Turning once again to the reminiscences of John Henderson in his letter of 1898, we find out how he became acquainted with the mysterious foreign gentleman and how Henneman revealed the secret of his activities:

> …to our great delight my friend Harrison, myself, and the Chemist's assistant, Tom Malone, were invited to spend an evening with him, when he showed us all the nature of his occupation and explained what he was engaged in endeavouring to accomplish.
>
> After this there was no further mystery about it, we were all pretty frequent visitors to his Studio, used to constantly sit for our portraits, and help him preparing his papers, arranging the Camera, a rather ponderous affair, and doing all we could to assist in the work.

Called upon to give an account of his time at the Establishment on a number of occasions and writing some fifty years after these events, it is not surprising that Henderson's memory is a little inconsistent on dates and details, but his letters do provide a fascinating and very human insight into the times. In a letter to his son 'Charley', dated 1892, Henderson expanded on his relationship with Henneman:

> After I had known him some months we got very friendly and on early Summer mornings we used to go rowing up the River [Thames]. I then discovered he had a keen eye for beautiful scenery, and on one occasion he casually observed 'I shall get you to help me some day to take some of these views'. Of course I said I could not draw, but he remarked he could take views without pencil or brush, and then disclosed to me the nature of his occupation and asked me to visit him the following Sunday, knowing that my then working hours were 14 per day and Sunday the only time I had a little leisure. Of course I went and was rather astonished at the sight his Studio presented. His cat and dog, himself, a large variety of Busts, Statuettes, and various articles in every variety of position appeared in various shades of brown on hundreds of sheets of paper; he had then done nothing away from home. In a few months we had become close friends. I was useful to him in carrying on a rather large correspondence with various people. This I mostly did late in the evening after business was over, but when he became a good customer to Lovejoy and the old man found out all about him, he occasionally allowed me to go down to write for him a whole evening...

Henderson and his friend Alfred Harrison were still employed by Lovejoy so at the beginning they were only able to work at the Establishment on a part-time basis, mainly in the evenings and at weekends. From his own account we can see that Henderson's main contribution was with correspondence and secretarial work. Henneman's mastery of foreign languages was impressive but, as Henderson noted, his written English was poor: 'he was rather deficient in English, and as I soon became known to him, he was glad of my help in assisting him with his growing correspondence'. In those letters that

Henneman wrote without Henderson's help, spelling and grammar could be haphazard, as we will see. The effect is rather charming and perhaps gives us an impression of his accent and spoken English.

Harrison seems to have been more involved with the practical side of the business, preparing paper and printing the photographs; Henneman also mentions his employment of a 'boy' who assisted in general duties. Henderson and Harrison's friend, Thomas Augustine Malone, was another part-time member of the team. He had met Henneman when, as an assistant in a chemist's shop, he had served him over the counter with chemical supplies.

They were a group of relatively young men: Henneman was in his early thirties, his assistants in their twenties and Talbot in his forties. They were all friends, and judging by the tone of their reminiscences and given Henneman's reputation for easy-going humour, the atmosphere at the Establishment must have been one of fun as well as hard work. They were full of enthusiasm and pioneering spirit, working at the cutting edge of this new process. But the work must also have demanded days of repetitive labour, sensitizing hundreds of sheets of paper by hand, exposed to chemical fumes and locked in the darkroom.

After the first eight months of production, Henneman had billed Talbot for 10,400 photographs. This was mass production, but the flow of work was erratic. Despite this impressive output of prints, Henneman was finding it difficult to justify the continued loan of the servants from Lacock. He wrote to Talbot on 31 May 1844:

Sir

Do not you think I better part with either Murray or Porter for I have not sufficient to do to emploi <u>one les</u> two and of course it is very expensive to me to keep them when I get nothing, coming in as at present, and I do not see any prospect to have suficient to do to inploy them <u>both</u>, beside the boy...

The 'business model' for the Establishment must have necessitated identifying, perhaps for the first time, a range of commercial uses to which photography could be put. Prints were produced for sale in bookshops, print shops and stationers, destined for framing and mounting on walls as works of art or mounting and storing in collectors' print cabinets. George Lovejoy's library and bookshop was one of the main retailers of Talbotypes and his window had mounted prints on display. Collectors and art lovers could have photographs made of paintings, sculptures, maps and engravings, for pleasure but also for documentation and insurance purposes, and valuable documents could be copied for legal reasons. Commissions to take portraits were an obvious demand but estate owners would also pay Henneman to take photographs of their grand houses, gardens and scenic views of the landscape. Photographic prints entitled 'Studies from nature' were produced for sale as an inspiration and aid to artists.

Amateur photographers were also encouraged. Henneman provided materials and tuition in the art: the Establishment offered private lessons in the practice of photography and advertised for sale pre-sensitised iodised paper for making 'Sun Pictures' at the cost of three shillings for five sheets, or two shillings and sixpence to 'Licensees'. A label printed for the packaging of the paper had a 'notice to purchasers':

> This Paper is prepared for the convenience of *Amateurs*, who *engage* to use the same *bona fide for purposes of amusement only*. Persons wishing to make a commercial or professional use of the Art can take out a License from the Patentee. *All applications for Licenses to be addressed to* Mr. Henneman, *Reading*.

Another important application for photography that had enormous potential was that of book illustration. With the negative process making it possible to make multiple copies of an image, it also became possible to paste individual positive prints into documents.

In his letter of 31 May 1844, Henneman discusses a project he was working on for the Walters, an important local family:

– I went to Mr Walter the other day but owing to the weather I did not get such good results as I expected wyl there I took another Negative of the Busts and Mr Walter is very much pleased with the result Mr Lovejoy advised me not to accept any thing if they offer it to mee thinking it will be more to the advantage for the Calotype, he thinks if <u>you</u> would make him a present of a coppy of your work telling him you heard tru me that he takes a great interest in the matter would have a good effect – I here with inclose you a coppy of the last I took and send him som today – the coppies I send him are rather better than yours the negative I did not boil for fear of getting to bad a ground like the others –

The weather has and is still very bad and not fit for <u>negatives</u> I hope your camera will soon arrive from Paris…

John Henderson had accompanied Henneman to Bearwood House and in another of his letters, written in 1898, he recalled:

It was about this time Mr Fox Talbot made it known that it was not his intention to take any steps to secure to himself any advantages he might derive from his discovery, and one day meeting our County Member, Mr John Walter the chief proprietor of the 'Times'… who was a constant visitor at Lovejoys, he explained the whole thing to him, and within a short period an article appeared in the columns of the 'Times' making the process known, and a free gift to the whole world.

Henneman & I were sent over to Bearwood to take copies of a beautiful Marble bust of Miss Catherine Walter, whose recent death had caused great grief to all who knew the Family. I much regret I did not retain copies of this beautiful work…

The Mr Walter referred to in Henneman's and Henderson's letters was the owner and editor of *The Times* newspaper who lived in a grand house on the Bearwood estate at Sindlesham,

CATHERINE MARY WALTER
BORN DECEMBER II ᵀᴴ MDCCCXIX
DIED JANUARY XVI ᵀᴴ MDCCCXLIV

Memorial booklet
for Catherine Walter

halfway between Reading and Wokingham. John Walter was the middle of three generations of Walters who owned *The Times*. He was an innovator and had been responsible for the introduction of steam printing to the newspaper industry in 1814. Walter was a familiar figure in Reading and a regular customer at Lovejoy's Library. Tragically, Walter's daughter Catherine Mary had died in January 1844, and her grieving father decided to publish privately a memorial booklet written by his son, also called John, who in turn later became owner and editor of *The Times*. As a young woman, Catherine had sat for a portrait bust carved in white marble, and Henneman was commissioned to make a photograph of the sculpture and produce multiple copies as a frontispiece for the booklet. The photograph was taken as a profile of the bust, printed out at approximately 57×75 mm ($2\frac{1}{4} \times 3$ inches) and pasted into the document by hand. Entitled *Record of the Death Bed of C.M.W.*, the text was printed by Gilbert & Riving in London and published in June 1844.

Although its circulation was very limited, this modest and rather sad booklet has the significance of being arguably the first published document in the world to be illustrated by photography. It demonstrated that photography had the potential to be used for illustrating books.

The Pencil of Nature

Competition that challenged the monopoly of the Reading Establishment was not long in coming. 'Daguerreomania' had not invaded Britain accompanied by the same euphoria as in France but Daguerreotype studios were opening up in many towns and cities. An article in the *Reading Mercury* of 4 May 1844 announced the availability of licences to set up studios in Berkshire:

> Mr. Beard, the patentee of the daguerreotype process, announces his wish to dispose of the agency for this county of this recent discovery in the arts. Of the faithfulness of portraiture by this means there can be no question, and we understand that the objections originally made to the peculiar hue of these pictures is now quite obviated. The speculation may prove profitable if the party is skilful in philosophical experiment. We lately alluded to the Calotype process, which is very effectively managed by Mr. Henneman at present a resident in this town. We hear that he is now publishing a work which will be illustrated by Calotype pictures, produced by the rays of light. The late brilliant sky and clear atmosphere have been most favourable for these processes.

The 'Mr. Beard' referred to as the patentee was Richard Beard, a business entrepreneur who had realised the huge potential of photographic portraiture. In 1841, Beard had bought the patent rights for the Daguerreotype in England, Wales and the Colonies and had opened the first public portrait studio in London. People flocked to have their picture taken – there was no end to the public's vanity – and it was a great success.

But it is the reference in the article to the publication of a book to be illustrated by calotypes that is of the greatest significance. This was a project that had been occupying Talbot's thoughts for some years, and indeed this publication might well have been the motivation and principal reason for setting up the

Reading establishment in the first place. As we have seen, Talbot had realised early on that the mass duplication of an image via the negative would open up enormous possibilities for the use of photography in book illustration. Yet he was acutely aware that the public had fallen in love with the Daguerreotype rather than his less glamorous prints and must have felt a deep frustration, knowing the true importance of his process. Writing to Sir John Herschel in December 1839, Talbot mentioned his ideas about book illustration:

> Although the perfection of the French method [of Photography] cannot be surpassed in some respects; yet in others the English is decidedly superior. For instance in the capability of multiplication of copies, & therefore of publishing a work with photographic plates.

Now Talbot needed a vehicle to explain its potential to the world, and there could be nothing better than a practical demonstration – producing hundreds of identical copies of a book full of his best photographs and showing the huge diversity of subject matter that was suitable for this new art: landscape, architecture, portraiture, still life, documentation. He would give his book the poetic title *The Pencil of Nature*.

This book would involve the production of photographs on a scale never attempted before. It required a 'factory' and someone who could oversee the work on a daily basis – and for whom it would provide a steady income. This was to be the core of the Establishment's business and provide most of the workload – all the other activities were important but not central. Talbot had already made hundreds of negatives but the first task was to decide on the structure of the book and the subject areas to illustrate, and then he would select the best images to be printed.

Right from the start, Talbot's idea was to publish his book in monthly parts. This was a practical solution to the problem of producing the large number of photographs needed

– the pressure on production could be spread over a longer period. Initially Henneman and Talbot intended to include fifty images in total, inserted in six parts, each issued with a variable number of five to ten prints, but the detailed plans for the book changed over time. Talbot had already been in discussion with the publisher Longman, Brown, Green, & Longmans of Paternoster Row, London over proposals for an illustrated book of his photographs of cathedrals. They now agreed to publish *The Pencil of Nature*, and in February 1844 publicity started to appear in their monthly list. In a prospectus sheet published in March, Longmans proclaimed: 'This is the first work ever published with photographic plates, that is to say, plates or pictures executed by Light alone, and not requiring for their formation any knowledge of drawing in the Operation. '

The idea of using the photograph itself to a illustrate a book by actually pasting the print onto the page was still a radical one. Even those involved with photography found it difficult to abandon the notion that a photograph was merely a source of reference to be copied by the engraver onto the surface of a woodblock, copper plate or drawn onto a lithographic stone for printing in the traditional way. It was hard for people to grasp the idea that with the negative, photography could be a form of printing itself. In a letter dated February 1843 to a William Snow Harris concerning a friend of Harris's who had a proposal for a book, Talbot tried to explain:

By the way, will you allow me to ask why your friend proposes to go to the great expense of having the drawings [photogenic drawings] engraved, when the process itself is capable of furnishing an unlimited number of copies, all facsimiles of each other, and at an expense I should think far inferior to that of Engraving.

The Calotype process dispenses not only with the draughtsman but also with the engraver & the copperplate printer. It executes the whole itself. The picture I believe to be quite permanent. A month's exposure to daylight at a window produces no effect on them, for they seem to have the same fixity as a printed page.

By June 1844 the first part of *The Pencil of Nature* was published. In an advertising leaflet Longmans announced:

JUST PUBLISHED.

PART I.

OF

THE PENCIL OF NATURE

BY

H. FOX TALBOT, ESQ.

THE NEW ART OF PHOTOGRAPHY was announced to the world almost simultaneously in France and England, at the commencement of the year 1839, by Mr. Daguerre and by the author of the present work. The processes employed were at first kept secret, but when they became known they were found to be exceedingly different. The French method, which has received the name of the Daguerreotype, is executed upon plates of polished silver, while paper is employed in the English process. The Daguerreotype is now well known to the public, having been extensively used for taking portraits from the life, while the English art (called PHOTOGENIC DRAWING, or the CALOTYPE) has been hitherto chiefly circulated in private societies, and is consequently less generally known.

It has been thought, therefore, that a collection of genuine specimens of the art, in most of its branches, cannot fail to be interesting to a large class of persons who have hitherto had no opportunity of seeing any well-executed specimens. It must be understood that the plates of the work now offered to the public are the pictures themselves, obtained by the action of light, and not engravings in imitation of them. This explanation is necessary, because some well-executed engravings have been published in France in imitation of

Photography, but they want the character of truth and reality which that art so eminently possesses. ... The plates of the present work will be executed with the greatest care, entirely by optical and chemical processes. It is not intended to have them altered in any way, and the scenes represented will contain nothing but the genuine touches of Nature's pencil.

It is proposed to publish the Work in Ten or Twelve Monthly Parts, in Royal quarto, price Twelve Shillings each, each Part containing Five Plates, with descriptive letter-press.

The present Number includes some account of the Author's first discovery of the Art.

In the event, the ten to twelve monthly parts proved to be too ambitious and *The Pencil of Nature* was published rather erratically in six parts between June 1844 and April 1846. The total number of prints issued was only twenty-four. Each of the six parts contained a commentary on the photographs by Talbot, and the number of prints in each part varied from five in Part 1 (price 12 shillings), seven in Part 2 (price 21 shillings), and three in Parts 3 to 6 (price 7 shillings and sixpence). The images were carefully selected from the hundreds of prints Talbot had taken to demonstrate the variety of subject matter and applications suitable for photography, featuring architecture, still life, figure compositions, botanical specimens and copies of works of art. The prints pasted into the book varied in size from approximately 130 mm square (5 × 5 inches) to 180 × 230 mm (7 × 9 inches). Talbot's text discussed the composition of the photographs, the position of the camera, effects of lighting and, where appropriate, the historical background to the subjects as well as the technical aspects of taking the picture. Talbot was aware that the general public still did not understand photography and mistrusted claims as to how it was done. He felt obliged to insert a slip of paper into each volume with a note to the reader emphasising once again that the images were 'impressed by the agency of

Light alone, without any aid whatever from the artist's pencil. They are the sun-pictures themselves, and not, as some persons have imagined, engravings in imitation'.

The first part of *The Pencil of Nature* was published in June 1844 in an edition of approximately 200 copies, but fewer copies were produced for the later parts as some subscribers dropped out owing to the cost and the delays in publication. The book opens with Talbot's account of the events leading to the invention of his process. Talbot writes in a very direct and personal style; in places the account is touching and almost poetic yet practical, with precise details of technique and chemistry. The five prints were mounted on blank pages with a carefully ruled border and interspersed with Talbot's short written commentary, which varied in length between one and three pages. The pages measured approximately 305 × 240 mm (12 × 9 ½ inches). The first illustration is a view of the buildings of Queen's College in Oxford, and Talbot points out how well the details of texture and weathering of the surface of the stone have been captured. The next image is a view of boulevards in Paris, taken from a high window, giving a wide view of the street and rooftops and capturing the atmosphere of the scene in the afternoon sun. The third depicts a collection of 'articles of china' displayed in regimented rows on shelves, and Talbot comments that the photograph is more effective than a written inventory. Next is a selection of glass objects; here Talbot focuses on some of the technical issues and exposure times involved in taking the image. The last print is of a white marble sculpture – a bust of Patroclus – and here Talbot is concerned with the effects of lighting on the three-dimensional object.

Now that photography is part of our everyday lives, the modern viewer might consider many of these images dull and uninspiring, but at the time even such mundane images were a miracle. Still, as mentioned before, Talbot was

Henneman holding a copy of *The Pencil of Nature*

trying to demonstrate the versatility and wide application of photography as well as showing its beauty as a creative art. Many of the images reveal Talbot's artistic sensitivity and feeling for composition and explore the effects of light and shade. The first photograph in Part 2 of *The Pencil of Nature* is an arched doorway, deep in shadow, with a rustic broom propped against the wall – a simple but moving image. Talbot comments that:

> The chief object of the present work is to place on record some of the early beginnings of a new art. ... This is one of the trifling efforts of its infancy... . We have sufficient

authority in the Dutch school of art, for taking as subjects of representation scenes of daily and familiar occurrence. A painter's eye will often be arrested where ordinary people see nothing remarkable. A casual gleam of sunshine, or a shadow thrown across his path, a time-withered oak, or a moss-covered stone may awaken a train of thoughts and feelings, and picturesque imaginings.

Talbot was heavily involved with writing and organising the design and production of the book; Talbot's notebooks contain quotations for the supply of paper and binding. Longmans had agreed to publish the book 'on commission' for the author; Talbot funded the project and Longmans took ten per cent on sales. He had undertaken to deliver a finished product to Longmans ready for distribution while Henneman concentrated on the considerable task of printing the thousands of photographic illustrations needed. The text was printed letterpress from a generous size of metal type by J.H. Cox Brothers, 'printers to the honourable East-India Company' with whom Talbot had worked in the past, and he organised the London firm of bookbinders, Alfred Tarrant, to mount the photographs and bind the sections.

The elaborate design for the cover of *The Pencil of Nature* has been attributed to Owen Jones, the great designer and pattern-maker of the nineteenth century. In 1851, Jones was to take a leading role in the design and decoration of the Great Exhibition at the Crystal Palace, and in 1856 he was to publish his famous book *The Grammar of Ornament*, which has been a source of inspiration for generations of artists and designers ever since. In the 1840s, Jones illustrated a number of books, particularly on the subject of medieval illuminated manuscripts, published by Longmans and printed by chromolithography. The covers of the separate parts of *The Pencil of Nature* were printed in red and black by the same process, and the intricate gothic style is typical of Jones's work.

LONGMAN, BROWN, GREEN AND LONGMANS.

LONDON. 1844.

Owen Jones has another connection with Reading, as the designer of many of the Huntley & Palmers biscuit labels printed by the firm De La Rue – designs so distinctive and colourful that they helped to establish Huntley & Palmers as a world brand.

Most of the prints published in *The Pencil of Nature* were 'positive prints' produced directly from the negative in a printing frame exposed in daylight – rather than by developing a 'latent' image – but it proved harder than expected to print large quantities of photographs consistent in quality and colour. In the twentieth century, photographers had the advantage of electric light that could be controlled with absolute precision and commercially manufactured photographic paper that was standardized and reliable. Poor Henneman and his team in Reading in the 1840s were at the mercy of the unpredictable British climate and the necessity of making everything by hand. The strength of the sun, the passing of clouds, the need to rescue the printing frames from sudden downpours – all these factors affected exposure times, making the production of identical prints almost impossible. Small variations in the balance and quantities of chemicals used also produced subtly different tones to the prints – from a soft, warm sepia to a bluish tint. In his introductory remarks to *The Pencil of Nature*, Talbot was at pains to be open and frank about the difficulties:

> There is a point to which I wish to advert, which respects the execution of the following specimens. As far as respects the design, the copies are almost facsimiles of each other, but there is some variety in the tint which they present. This arises from a twofold cause. In the first place, each picture is separately formed by the light of the sun, and in our climate the strength of the sun's rays is exceedingly variable even in serene weather. When clouds intervene, a longer time is of course allowed for the impression of the picture, but it is not possible to reduce this to a matter of strict and accurate calculation.

> The other cause is the variable quality of the paper employed, even when furnished by the same manufacturers – some difficulties in the fabrication and in the sizing of the paper, known only to themselves, and perhaps secrets of the trade, have a considerable influence on the tone of colour which the picture ultimately assumes.

These tints, however, might undoubtedly be brought nearer to uniformity, if any great advantage appeared likely to result: but, several persons of taste having been consulted on the point, viz. which tint on the whole deserved preference, it was found that their opinions offered nothing approaching to unanimity, and therefore, as the process presents us spontaneously with a variety of shades of colour, it was thought best to admit whichever appeared pleasing to the eye, without aiming at an uniformity which is hardly attainable...

As Talbot points out, the quality of the paper used was crucial to the result of the process; finding a supplier of paper of consistent quality was one of their nagging problems. The surface of the paper, the raw materials and amount of size used and the even thickness and opacity of the paper were all variables that could affect the quality of the photographic print. The paper used for the negative had to be as translucent as possible when waxed − so preferably thin but retaining strength. George Lovejoy's stationery department was the source of much of the paper used − he could supply high quality writing paper. The best results were achieved with Whatman's 'Turkey Mill Paper' which had a smooth, even surface and also 'wet strength'; like most paper made in Britain at the time, it was sized with gelatin.

The vast majority of the photographs in *The Pencil of Nature* were taken by Talbot himself, but, as we have seen, Henneman did have to re-take certain images due to damage to the negatives. Handling the paper negatives − the unique master copies − could be problematic, as Talbot mentions in his text:

> ... a very great number of copies can be obtained in succession, so long as great care is taken of the original picture. But being only paper, it is exposed to various accidents; and should it be casually torn or defaced, of course no more copies can be made. A mischance of this kind having occurred to two

plates in our earliest number after many copies had been taken from them, it became necessary to replace them by others; and accordingly the Camera was once more directed to the original objects themselves, and new photographic pictures obtained from them, as a source of supply for future copies. But the circumstances of light and shade and the time of day, c. not altogether corresponding to what they were on a former occasion, a slightly different but not worse result attended the experiment. From these remarks, however, the difference which exists will be easily accounted for.

Now, once again, just for a short while, let us use our imagination and get a sense of what work at the Reading Establishment during the production of *The Pencil of Nature* might have been like as part of everyday life. (Much of the technical detail in the following chapter is based on an account of the Establishment's working methods by Thomas Malone, published in the *Liverpool and Manchester Photographic Journal* in 1857.)

A day in the life of the Establishment

Henneman wakes early despite the fact that he read late into the night; his book rests on a rickety tripod table next to the bed, beside the stub of a melted candle in its holder. His mind is racing with the problems he is facing in trying to keep up with the schedule for the project in hand. He knows how much Talbot depends on him and that adds to the pressure; he does not want to let down his old employer and friend – he owes him so much.

Suddenly he jumps out of bed – there is no point in fretting – and throws on his dressing gown. From the small landing, illuminated by early morning sun coming through the skylight, he noisily descends the narrow attic staircase. On the next floor down he enters the small sitting room, once a dormitory for the pupils of the school that used to occupy the building. The room is in darkness and he tentatively makes his way across the turkey carpet, carefully avoiding the card table in the middle of the room, on which the chess board and pieces still stand from last night's game. His face breaks into a slight smile as he suddenly recalls his triumph over Henderson whose King lies knocked over. Guided by a chink of light coming through the wooden shutters, he lifts the latch and opens them and the room floods with daylight. There is a smell of stale tobacco from the cigar stubs that litter the ashtrays so he raises the sash window to let in some fresh air. He leans out, takes a deep breath and looks down at the street and then up at the sky, pale blue with a covering of high, thin cloud. This is promising, perfect for a full day of printing. The expression on Henneman's face is one of relief: perhaps they can catch up on production. So many days in the last week have been dull and overcast, and two days were lost to rain. Henneman has become rather good at assessing the weather: he knows through bitter experience how critical it is for a good day's work. Blazing sun can be too powerful, but bright, diffused light with thin cloud is perhaps the best condition for printing as it gives them more control over the exposures.

As always, the room is cluttered with the untidy trappings of bachelor life. Books are piled on every available surface. A number of plaster busts are balanced on slightly wobbly pedestals, and a copy of Canova's sensual *Three Graces* takes pride of place. Many of the objects are here for no other purpose than to serve as props for his photographic studies. His desk is covered with ledgers and paperwork – before their game commenced he and Henderson were working on correspondence. A side table is piled with photographic prints held down by a large magnifying lens. A folded copy of the *Reading Mercury* lies on the seat of the armchair, half hidden by the smoking cap with its trailing gold tassel, a lovingly embroidered leaving present from Sarah, one of the maids at Lacock, for whom he feels an increasing fondness.

From the window Henneman looks across open land and gardens to the handsome terraced houses of Russell Street and down to the Oxford Road, where he can just see the new stone façade and bellcote of Holy Trinity Church, which has recently been completed by John Billing, a local architect and builder. He is distracted by the clanking of milk churns as a dairy cart trundles into view. The 'boy' (as Henneman's most junior assistant is known) opens the front door and runs across to the man pushing the cart holding out a large jug. The milkman, William White from Castle Street, reaches for the tin measure hanging from the rim of the nearest churn, dips it into the fresh milk and pours the contents into the jug.

The boy has already been at work for over an hour: he has stoked the fire in the kitchen range and lit a new fire under the large copper boiler in the wash house – they will need a good supply of hot water for the day's tasks. Now, having returned to the kitchen, he places a big, blackened kettle onto the range to boil, ready for Henneman's breakfast coffee. Henneman is very fussy about his coffee and has taught the boy how to make it in the continental way.

Henneman himself now climbs the stairs back to his attic bedroom. The boy has placed a jug of water at his door which he takes into the room and pours into the blue willow-patterned basin of the washstand. Henneman takes care of his ablutions and dress. He splashes the cold water under his arms, towels himself down and pulls on a linen shirt.

Tucking the long tails between his thighs and tottering on one leg, he slips first one foot and then the other into his trousers and finally pulls his braces over his shoulders. He deftly trims his side-whiskers with a pairs of scissors, then studies his face in the mottled and cracked old mirror above the basin. Anxious to get on, he decides to leave shaving until tomorrow. He fiddles for a while tying his neck-cloth and then selects his favourite waistcoat, cut from a rather flamboyant and colourful fabric – there is just a little bit of the dandy in him. He enjoys getting stuck in with the practical work of processing and printing, but these days he has to keep respectably clean and tidy to greet and serve the clients. As he picks the odd dog hair off his jacket, he can hear the happy yelping of his faithful hound as he is let out into the yard.

Henneman descends to the ground floor which, except for the kitchen, is now entirely given over to the photographic workshop. There are several darkrooms: the room for processing calotype negatives has to be kept in total darkness, but other processes are less sensitive to light and need only be protected from direct sunlight. Grabbing a plate and a knife from the dresser, Henneman enters the little larder with its cool slate and marble shelves and cuts himself a piece of cheese. The butter is getting a little rancid – it has been warm recently and it is difficult to keep things cold. He cuts off a few slices from the fresh crusty loaf that the boy has collected on his walk to work.

The boy's family are poor and live in one of the slum dwellings in a yard off Friar Street. He sleeps with three of his brothers in a lumpy bed in an attic room and has to be very careful not to wake them when he crawls over their sleeping bodies – he is usually the first to leave the house. He knows just how lucky he is to have a job with such educated people and is anxious always to be on time. He looks forward to getting the bread at Charles Moss's shop in St Mary's Butts – he can smell the freshly baked loaves as he approaches. Old Moss is always grumpy in the mornings but the shop is warm and he usually gives the boy a left-over bun knowing that is all he will have for breakfast.

After his hasty repast and a welcome romp with his dog who now sits obediently at his side, Henneman briefs the boy about the day's activities. He wants Harrison to concentrate on preparing a batch of paper while he and Malone finish printing the last images for the next part of *The Pencil*. He pulls on the fancy chain of his pocket watch and checks the time; it is quarter past eight. He is keen to make the most of the good weather; he opens the front door and anxiously looks down the street to see if there is any sign of his assistants. His neighbour, Mr Maddeford, cheerfully doffs his hat in passing on the way to his clock-making workshop nearby. Henneman catches a glimpse of Harrison and Malone in the distance at the end of Hosier Street; he waves and goes back indoors, leaving the door ajar. Moments later he hears Harrison and Malone crossing the threshold engaged in loud banter. The topic is their rivalry over the University boat race that has just been held over the new Putney–Mortlake course – Harrison supports Oxford and Malone Cambridge. Removing their top hats and frock coats, the two men roll up their sleeves ready to get to work as Henneman greets them and gives them their instructions.

Harrison goes into the preparation room, which has a bench along the wall lined with ceramic dishes. Henneman insisted on investing in these as the old troughs they used at Lacock in the early days – made by the estate carpenter from oak planking and sealed with bitumen – often leaked and were difficult to keep clean. Harrison's task today is to prepare a batch of sensitised paper – some for sale to amateur photographers, some for printing Talbot's negatives. Yesterday he collected packets containing several hundred sheets of best quality letter-writing paper from his old employer, Lovejoy. This took some while as he could not avoid his old customer Miss Mitford who wanted to gossip, and Lovejoy himself collared him to rant about the state of the water in the town and his plans for reform. Harrison misses the celebrated literary folk who frequent Lovejoy's Library – he used to enjoy boasting to his friends of his connections with high society.

First, Harrison has to make up a solution of salt water. Taking an apron from the hook on the back of the door he shouts to the boy to bring a flagon of distilled water, the preparation of which is yet another of the boy's many tasks. The water from the hand pump by the stone sink in the kitchen is often polluted and discoloured and not suitable unless treated. Harrison reaches for a large china milk pail, scoops salt from a small sack on the shelf above and heaps it on the pan of a set of scales. The salt, too, is the result of the boy's labours – he crushes and grinds lumps of rock salt in a mortar until it is fine enough to dissolve easily. Harrison uses one or two ounces (30 to 60 grams) of salt to a gallon (four and a half litres) of water, depending on the quality of the paper – experience has taught him to judge the exact amounts carefully. Once the salt has dissolved he pours the solution into one of the dishes. He opens the first packet of paper and checks the top sheets, holding them up to the light to see if he can spot any impurities. Turkey Mill paper is usually of high quality but Harrison knows that any fragment of metal or broken button from the shredded and pulped cotton rags that have found their way into the paper can cause problems. He immerses several sheets in the solution for about two minutes, then removes them one by one and lays them on the sheet of glass on a table beside the sink. He uses his pad of soft, smooth cloth to dab both sides of each sheet to remove excess salt water. Now he takes the stack of damp sheets next door, where the boy has lit a small fire in the grate which is just beginning to take the chill off the room. Although it is a warm day the room needs additional heat to dry the sheets as quickly as possible. Wooden drying racks have been built against one wall of the room and lined with paper by the boy who has already collected the dried salted paper that Harrison soaked at the end of the previous day.

Next, Harrison sensitises the dried sheets. He finds an empty glass jar and rinses it with water from the pump. From the chemical cupboard he selects a large flask with a pasted label reading 'ammonia nitrate of silver' in copperplate lettering. This solution has been prepared by Charles Bewley, a chemist in London Street, although sometimes he also buys supplies from Ford & Miller or George Cooper in Market Place. However, Bewley's solution has been found to produce 'smoky' and cold slate-coloured prints. Talbot has advised adding dilute nitric acid to the solution which helps to clear it and results in warmer tones, although if too much acid is used the prints come out with a vulgar orange or reddish colour. The perfect tint they have agreed on is a good, rich, velvety tone, but the exact quantities and proportions seem to vary depending on conditions and the paper being used. This problem frequently drives Harrison mad, and although he has made up the solution many times he is always conscious how 'hit or miss' the outcome is. None of them truly understand how the acid works or why paper from one manufacturer needs less salt and produces a better colour than that from another, and Harrison can only rely on his experience.

He pours the solution into another dish. One by one he floats the sheets of salted paper on the surface of the ammonia nitrate solution, almost immediately picks them up by two corners and allows excess liquid to drip back into the dish, making sure that the reverse side remains free of the solution. He then lays the damp sheets onto clean lining paper on another rack. He used to paint on the solution with a broad brush and still does if preparing a small batch of paper as it is more economical, but this often leads to untidy brush marks feathering out at the edges of the paper, whereas floating the sheets produces a more even coating right to the edges.

It is rather tedious and repetitive work, which Harrison will be doing for most of the day. In addition, he gets brown stains on his fingers from contact with the silver nitrate, and however rigorously he scrubs his hands he cannot get rid of it. His friends in the beer house rag him endlessly about the amount he must be smoking.

The day is warming up so the sheets will dry naturally fairly quickly, but Harrison takes them into the drying room just to make sure they are free of any moisture. This first batch of sensitised paper is for use today but his next batch will be put between boards in an old screw press that stands on a table in the corner of the drying room. Under pressure and away from light, the paper will be fine for use tomorrow or the next day.

While Harrison has been working on preparing the paper, Henneman and Malone have been looking through the selection of negatives made by Talbot on his last visit to Reading to decide which ones to print next. The negatives were made using the calotype process, which develops a latent image, but the prints taken from them will be photogenic drawings (or 'sun pictures', or salt prints) printed directly onto the paper

Harrison has sensitised. The boy has been cleaning the printing frames and polishing the glass – it was windy yesterday as well as showery and the glass got dusty and spattered with raindrops as they rushed to bring the frames inside.

They lay out the negatives on tables. Four or five are destined for *The Pencil,* but they need to fill the racks outside with batches of about twenty-five frames to be efficient, so the other negatives they will print are for colleagues and amateur photographers, with a fee being charged for the service. They hold each negative up to the window to assess the density of the image which will critically affect the exposure time. The reasonable light today is ideal for the denser negatives, which are slow to print on a dull day. They have found that exposure times can vary from ten minutes to over thirty minutes, twenty minutes being an average. As they go through the negatives, each is placed in one of the folders marked with different estimated exposure times so that it can be put out on the racks at the right time.

The paper of the negatives is translucent like tracing paper: it has been waxed using another time-consuming and delicate process. On a slab of stone that has been heated on top of the kitchen range and then rubbed all over with a block of beeswax, a developed paper negative is sandwiched between two clean sheets of blotting paper. Meanwhile, the metal bricks for inserting into the box iron through a sliding door at the back of it have been heating on the stove. By ironing over the covering sheet of blotting paper, the softened beeswax from the stone is drawn into the paper negative. Ironing the saturated negative between sheets of clean paper removes surplus beeswax.

Having selected the best negatives and worked out which ones need more or less exposure in the sunlight, Henneman and Malone gather up the folders and take them to where the boy has stacked the frames. Having collected fresh sensitised paper from the drying room, they assemble the printing frames: the sensitised paper is placed centrally on the velvet-covered base board, the negative – smaller than the printing paper – comes next, and finally the glass sheet goes on top. A frame is fitted around the glass and screwed to the base board to ensure perfect contact between the negative and the sensitised paper.

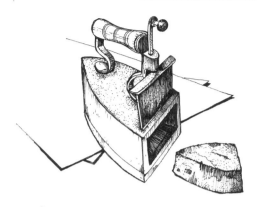

Box iron and heated metal brick

The men carefully instruct the boy about the sequence of exposure times. An accurate clock is kept just inside the door of the conservatory and the boy makes a note of the timings in a book he keeps in the pocket of his apron. The boy carries the first batch of frames outside and arranges them in rows on the racks. He will spend the rest of the daylight hours rushing to and fro, moving the frames along the rack and bringing out new ones in turn, as well as keeping an eye on the fires and the supply of water for the processing rooms. He will be kept on his feet but is well aware of all his responsibilities – if he gets in a muddle he can ruin the day's work. His predecessor made expensive mistakes and did not last long in the job.

Malone now collects the first batch of exposed frames from the boy and takes them inside for washing and fixing. As the boy is busy putting out the next lot of frames, Malone takes a large pail to the copper boiler in the washhouse and draws off some hot water. He pours it into one of the rectangular tin dishes in the fixing room, tests the temperature of the water and then rinses the positive prints that he has taken out of the frames to remove excess nitrate and any superficial deposits. Earlier, Malone has mixed a fresh solution of 'fix' – hyposulphate of soda, known as 'hypo' – consisting of about one part of a saturated solution of the salt in ten parts of water. This is enough for the twenty-five small prints – each on average 7 x 9 inches (18 x 23 cm) that he has ready. The hypo is diluted with water from the copper, as hot as his hands will bear, and now the rinsed prints are immersed in the hot 'fix' for about ten minutes. Finally, Malone lifts them out and puts them into the first of three dishes filled with clean water that are set out on a bench against one wall of the room. It has taken three gallons of water (nearly 14 litres) to fill them, brought in pails from the pump by the boy earlier in the morning. The prints are moved on from one dish to the next and thus washed in progressively cleaner water (or as clean as it can be, given the state of Reading's water supply). To check that the water in the last dish is clear of 'fix', Malone periodically dips his finger into the water and tastes it: it was John Herschel who

The boy putting the printing frames out for exposure

passed on the tip that hyposulphate tastes sweet and assured everyone that this is a safe way to check for traces of it in the water.

Malone pours the remaining hyposulphate of soda down the sink (it is best to use fresh solution for each batch). He takes each print in turn out of the final wash and places it between sheets of blotting paper to remove excess moisture before taking the batch into the drying room. They have recently discovered that the prints take on a particularly pleasing tone if they are dried close to the fire, and ever since they produced the prints of the memorial bust of John Walter's daughter, they have frequently gone over the prints with a hot iron. So later in the day, when he has accumulated enough prints, Malone will do a spell of ironing.

And so the day progresses. It has been fairly relentless, with only the occasional break to grab a bite to eat. Henneman has had to deal with a few awkward customers and has also tackled a pile of paperwork, invoices and bills, which he hates – he is passionate about the creative side of photography, but not about the boring business side of the work. Once Harrison, Malone and the boy have cleaned up and left, Henneman sits by the dying embers of the fire in the drying room, surrounded by the day's output. It has gone well, as well as he had hoped, and they have caught up on production.

He picks up the letter from Talbot that came during the afternoon. (Henneman is amazed at the regularity of the deliveries – the postal service has had a big impact on his business and although the penny post has only been operating for a few years, he has come to rely on it.) He breaks the red seal, unfolds the letter and scans the contents: it is only Talbot letting him know about his next visit to Reading. Henneman lies back in the chair. His housekeeper will be dropping in soon with a pie for his supper; after that he will reply to Talbot's letter and perhaps write one to his sweet Sarah. He falls asleep.

Photogenic

by Lesley Saunders

*'In those very early days of photography when subjects had to stay still
for so long, a conveniently sleeping subject was perfect for a sharp print.'*

Nicolaas asleep the perfect pose
stilled life jacketless right hand deep
in thought left hand on thigh forefinger
pointing out of the frame to a dream

of light its action on paper an art of
great singularity but no end of grief
leaving its impression upon the material
body obscure & lucid only by long

exposure rendered in iodide of potassium
nitrate of silver bath of salt chloride of silver
manifest in these intimate halftones at last
a shadow-haunting beauty destined to fade.

In the spirit of Two Rivers Press let us pause for a moment
and read the poem above by Lesley Saunders who was
moved by the image of Nicolaas Henneman asleep in a chair.
Lesley is a local poet and has published widely, including a
volume of poems entitled *Cloud Camera* which were inspired
by her fascination with scientific instruments and objects. It
was published by Two Rivers Press in 2012.

Opposite:
This photograph of Henneman asleep is attributed to Talbot, who
is thought to have taken it in *c*. 1845. It is a salt print from a calotype
negative.

Reception and promotion

Despite the considerable problems encountered in the mass production of photographs, Talbot and his team had triumphed with the publication of the first number of *The Pencil of Nature*. With all its faults, this pioneering publication was generally well received by the critics and the public and was beginning to achieve Talbot's aim: to demonstrate the potential of his process. A writer in *The Critic: The London Literary Journal* commented that he was in doubt whether photography was an art or a science:

> ... it will be eagerly sought by lovers of both... . And it is a great recommendation of it, that for a few pence a faithful representation can be taken of any place or object it may be desirable to preserve... . Meanwhile, The Pencil of Nature affords abundant evidence of the utility of the Calotype process — to the traveller, in fixing the scenes he visits; to the naturalist, in procuring a faithful representation of living and inanimate objects; and to the world at large in preserving the features of those dear to us. Nor should its value to the artist be unnoticed; since the limnings of The Pencil of Nature demonstrate the importance of a due knowledge and observance of the distribution of light and shade in delineating every object, and the compatibility of breadth of effect with minuteness of detail in a picture. The triumph of Titian and the Old Masters is complete indeed, when Nature herself produces pictures exemplifying the soundness of the principles on which they painted... . We heartily recommend this work to our readers, and we shall look with interest for the succeeding numbers of it.

The magnitude of Talbot's achievement was also recognised by a review in the *Literary Gazette*:

> We have only to add another tribute of our applause to that gentleman [Talbot] for the skill with which he has overcome

the difficulties of a first attempt at photographic publication, and the excellence he has already attained in executing his designs...

The journal *Art-Union* particularly praised the view of Queen's College, Oxford, which was the first plate of the first part, describing it as

the most perfect that can be conceived; the minutest detail is given with a softness that cannot be imitated by any artistic manipulation... the whole is melted in and blended into form by the mysterious agency of natural chemistry.

More locally, the *Reading Mercury* was impressed by the quality of the production:

A very beautiful Work has been commenced... . The first number of it contains very exquisite impressions from different subjects originally reflected in a Camera Obscura: the letter-press is illuminated, and the whole is of a very costly description, several thousand impressions have been literally printed or painted by the sun's rays, in the last few months, at the laboratory of a scientific gentleman in this town, engaged in getting up this work.

The *Athenaeum* published a lengthy article on the first two issues of the book and noted the significance of the publication:

...photography has already enabled us to hand down to future ages a picture of the sunshine of yesterday, or a memorial of the haze of to-day... . The 'Pencil of Nature' is the first attempt at photographic publication... . The experiment of photographically-illustrated books is now before the world; and all who see Mr. Talbot's production will be convinced that the promise of the art is great, and its utility and excellence, in many respects, of a high order...

However, there were less positive comments from the same journal in June 1845, when a review appeared of Part 3 of *The Pencil of Nature*, which had just been published:

...although Mr. Fox Talbot's specimens are of very interesting character, we are not yet satisfied that the problem of photo-graphic publication is solved. The irregular appearance of 'The Pencil of Nature', the small number of pictures those parts contain, and the high price at which they are sold, all prove that the labour consequent on the production of photographs is too great to render them generally useful for the purposes of illustration.

Despite all the vision and hard work that went into the book, the publication only just about broke even. Publication had been erratic and the number of copies sold fell short of expectations. Because of delays in bringing out the later parts, Henneman often appealed to Talbot for more orders for prints to keep production up. However, the significance of *The Pencil of Nature* went beyond the quality of the book itself and its commercial success – the historian Beaumont Newhall has compared its importance in the history of photography 'to that of the Gutenberg Bible in printing'.

Despite the pressure of producing around 4300 prints for *The Pencil of Nature* Henneman had made some efforts to promote Talbot's process and the work of the Establishment. On 25 January 1845 he wrote to Talbot about the preparations for his talk at the Mechanics' Institution, which he appears to have been somewhat reluctantly forced into:

I have at last consented to give a Lecture to the members of the Reading Scientific Institution on Photography in conse-quence of a gentleman expressing his intention of doing so, who I am sure knew nothing of the Subject, but what he had gleaned from newspapers. If you will oblige me with a copy of 'Some account of the art of Photogenic Drawing' and any other papers, also the Literary Gazette containing the first notice of your invention they will be of great assistance to me, as I intend reading the Lecture. I think I had better make some few extracts from them. If it meets your approbation I think I shall have an opportunity of getting it noticed in the *Times*. Do you not think I had better do so? The Secretary of the Institution, who is an intelligent Scientific man, has kindly offered me his assistance on the occasion. I have also asked some information of Mr. Keates on the Daguerreotype to which I shall be obliged to allude, any further information you can favor me with will be very thankfully received. The Lecture will not take place till March, still I shall be greatly obliged by your granting my request as early as convenient.

It seems that a rival Daguerreotype studio had finally been set up in Reading, run by a Mr Keates. The Mechanics' Institution had recently been opened in purpose-built premises next door to Lovejoy's Library in London Street. It had immediately become a focus for intellectual activity in the town. Lectures were wide-ranging in subject and the speaker list for the last quarter of 1844 included topics such as 'Thoughts on popular delusions', 'Light and polarized light', 'Antiquities of India', 'Genius of Shakespeare', 'The most distinguished female sovereigns of Europe', and a certain Mr Benjamin Cowderoy spoke on 'Electrography'.

Henneman's talk was received with great acclaim and a reviewer in the *Reading Mercury* was full of praise:

On Tuesday evening a lecture was delivered to members upon a new branch of discovery in the arts, 'Photography,' by Mr. Henneman... . This discovery, and the further improvements by the author, formed the subject of the lecture. Mr. H. described the principles and effects of this most singular art in terms which, not withstanding his being a native of another country, were clear, concise, and intelligible. He illustrated his description of the process by taking upon a sheet of sensitive prepared paper an impression made from a plaster cast, which was illuminated by an oxy-hydrogen flame, and which, by a lens, was reflected into a camera obscura. Mr. H. is a very skilful operator, and an agent of Mr. Talbot's in carrying out the beautiful results of this delightful art. We understand that the last improvement gives an impression in two seconds of time. The calotype portraits and views which were exhibited were most beautiful, rivaling the finest engravings and drawings. The lecture was received with great applause.

Talbot and Henneman had achieved a great deal but neither man had enough time, experience or aptitude for marketing or the administrative side of the business. One initiative they did take was to gain some free publicity by participating in a science exhibition held at the Mechanics' Institution in December 1845. This 'Polytechnic Exhibition and Bazaar' featured displays on many aspects of art, natural history and science, and an article describing the event appeared in the *Berkshire Chronicle* on 10 January 1846.

The immense collection of paintings, covering the sides of the large hall, and smaller paintings which cover the walls of the lecture-room, forming a smaller picture gallery, have proved highly interesting, particularly the specimens of the Talbotype and Daguerreotype, kindly contributed by Mr. Fox Talbot, Mr. Claudet, and Mr. Henneman. The papier maché stalls, fitted up most tastefully, and furnished by Mr. John Snare [the Reading printer who designed and produced the poster used on the inside cover of this book], have contained a most elegant display of new and highly finished goods in that department.

The splendid skull of a Ceylon elephant was on loan from Charles Havell, another member of the Havell family, and there was a 'Ladies' sale of goods'. It seems to have been a huge success: over 2500 visitors came in four days and it was suggested that the exhibition stay open for a further week. The paper particularly praised a Mr B. Cowderoy:

Façade of Mechanics' Institution in London Street
(now the Great Expectations public house & hotel)

> To Mr. B. Cowderoy, Honorary Secretary of the Institution…
> the public are greatly indebted; and the skill, taste and
> judgement the gentlemen [of the committee] have exhibited
> in the combination, arrangement and display of this beautiful
> repository of nature and art, receive what they richly deserve
> – the need of unqualified praise and unanimous admiration.

As the general lack of marketing remained one of the
weaknesses of the business at Russell Terrace, Talbot engaged
the services of Mr Benjamin Cowderoy, perhaps because of
his good reputation.

Cowderoy was an accountant and established businessman,
a broker for stocks and shares and an auctioneer and estate

agent who had been one of the speakers at the Mechanics' Institution. In the 1840s he had premises in London Street, not far from Lovejoy's Library. He was born in Reading in 1812 and, rather like George Lovejoy, grew up in a family of liberal political views. In later life he enjoyed recounting his pleasure at the passing of the Reform Bill of 1832 and the repeal of the Corn Laws in 1846. However, some memories were less joyful: he remembered as a child witnessing the public hanging of a gipsy for horse-stealing outside Reading gaol and it left a lasting harrowing impression. Later he was employed by one of the firms of iron-workers in the town who supplied material for the construction of the Great Western Railway.

Cowderoy was a good appointment. Energetic and motivated, he proved to be an effective organiser and tried to provide a sounder business footing for the Establishment. He set about promoting and increasing sales of individual prints, advising Talbot that he should encourage businesses to open accounts and proposing that he should actively seek out new outlets on a trial basis. Writing to Talbot on 30 April 1846, he reported:

I was in Town [London] yesterday with various printsellers. Ackerman was out of Town, but I had an interview with his Manager with whom I left a few specimens and who has promised to write me with Mr. A's determination. I opened Accounts with two Houses – Garner in Regent Street and Gibbs in Titchbourne Street. I also obtained information to guide me in selecting two or three good houses in the City with whom I hope to conclude arrangements the next time I am in Town. Ackerman in Regent Street declined on the ground of having no room for the pictures. He is certainly very full but I could see that the main reason was that Brooks had the precedence. I have received the Stamp from Brooks who asks for more <u>Trees</u> and Maltese Views – shall I supply him? … We should open Accounts in some 20 good Towns as well as with the London houses in order to make the trial a fair one. I go tomorrow to Oxford and Cheltenham and we can then decide on the other Towns to be taken I have given a small Stock to each of the two principal Houses here… . I have the letter from Bath – if the writer applies to me I will see if he can make a Journey answer I think it would be a good place to open two or three Accounts.

Ackerman eventually became a valuable outlet stocking Talbot's prints. The firm of Brooks mentioned in the letter was Henry Brooks, a publisher and printseller in New Bond Street who had had a special stamp made for marking Talbotypes and also a decorative chromolithographed label that he glued to the back of the prints.

The trip to Oxford and Cheltenham proved fruitful, and by the end of the year Cowderoy had made deals with outlets in Eton, Windsor, Southampton, Manchester, Northampton, Cambridge, Banbury, Oxford, Gloucester, Cheltenham and Birmingham. As mentioned in the letter, views of Malta were popular with the first overseas outlet that they had set up on the island. Reading remained an important outlet, with other businesses as well as Lovejoy's shop selling prints from the Establishment. On 22 July Cowderoy wrote to Talbot:

Mr Shipton on the promenade is our principal Agent [in Reading]. Mr Lovejoy is not many doors from him (–towards the High Street) is the other. You will perhaps drop into their Shops at your leisure. Mr Shipton has declined the offer of the positives of 6 local Views @ 1/6 each as proposed. Shall you take some views during your stay or will it still be requisite to send Henneman?

In the same letter Cowderoy proposed a trip to the Isle of Wight, anticipating the profit to be made from photographing places connected to Queen Victoria:

If the weather favored me I am sure I could bring a good stock of selling pictures from the Isle of Wight, if you think a week's excursion for the purpose worth while. At Southampton, Cowes, Portsmouth etc. famous opportunities offer for taking

Cover of the Art-Union journal

shipping. Osborne House, with its new Tower etc. would pay
for a Journey if one two or three good views of it were taken.
Cowderoy might well have been the initiator of another
ambitious promotional ploy – the inclusion of a free Talbotype
print in every copy of *The Art-Union Monthly Journal of the Arts*
for 1 June 1846. The journal had a circulation of around 7000
copies and to provide prints on that scale presented a huge
production challenge that must have tested the efficiency of
the Establishment to the limit. The prints inserted into the
journal were not all the same – a number of images were
used – but it must have been a tedious and repetitive task

for Henneman and his assistants. This was the first time a photographic image was published in a journal and made available to the general public *en masse*. *The Times* carried an advertisement for the journal:

> THE TALBOTYPE.–Sun Painting.–The ART–UNION for June will contain an example of the Talbotype, supplied to that Journal by the inventor, Fox Talbot, Esq., F.R.S.. Although the fame of this wonderful discovery has gone over the world, the number of those who have been as yet able to obtain an example of it is comparatively limited. This opportunity of possessing one cannot therefore fail to be taken advantage of, and the subscribers are requested to procure copies early. The Specimen will be accompanied by a history of the invention and a description of the process…

The accompanying editorial comment in the journal was very favourable; while recognising the qualities of the Daguerreotype and its popularity, it pointed out that Talbot's process had not been given the same exposure:

> … the Talbotype has been hitherto only circulated in private societies, and is, consequently, less generally known. We presume, however, that the circulation of the very large number of examples with which Mr Talbot has supplied us, will have the effect of making many thousands acquainted with it who had previously only heard of it as one of the wonders of the age… . In reducing the two inventions to a consideration of their real utilities, the preference must be given to the Talbotype. The invention of Daguerre was matured at its announcement… . On the other hand, the Talbotype, since it was first made known, has, through the unremitting labours and research of its inventor, been wonderfully improved…

This endorsement of Talbot's process was later tarnished by the fact that many of the prints distributed in the journal badly faded with time.

Cowderoy also spent time on negotiating licences for amateur and commercial use of the calotype process on behalf of Talbot. He tailored agreements for those wanting to specialise in areas such as portraiture and agreed the scope of the licence – local or national use – and the right to supply materials and equipment. Another of his responsibilities was to organise training courses for beginners. On 22 July 1846, Cowderoy used the back of an advertising sheet to write a letter to Talbot; the following extracts from the advertising copy give an indication of the charges:

For a License to an Amateur, *bona fide* for the purpose of amusement only … 1 Guineas

Ditto, with Personal Instructions, given at the Reading Establishment … 10 Guineas

(The instructions comprise Four Lessons, which may extend from 10 a.m. to 2 p.m. – and, if desired, are given in two portions, for the learner to practise in the interval)

An order for Iodised paper to the amount of three Guineas will entitle the purchaser to an Amateur's License *gratis.*

Where Five or more persons, in one Town, form a Class for instruction, an Artist is sent to teach them, at a small additional charge.

It is expected from Licensees, as one of the conditions of the License, (and which is at the same time an additional security for their success,) that they will purchase their iodised paper from the Reading Establishment: the manufacture of that article being secured by patent, and requiring very particular care and attention. The Prices are –

Best quality – Packets of 5 sheets for large Cameras … 4s.

Ditto, 10 sheets for small ditto… 2s.

Second quality – in similar Packets, at *one-fourth less.*

The Iodised Paper is warranted to keep any length of time in any climate, without change.

A complete set of Apparatus can be had *only* of Mr. B. Cowderoy, Reading, who has on hand a Stock of Cameras and Cases of Chemicals, adapted to every purpose. The prices are from 5 Guineas upwards. No others can be relied on. Cash payments.

This advertisement was only one of a number of promotional documents that Cowderoy produced. In around 1846 he commissioned a local printer, John Snare, to print a broadside, or poster, advertising Talbotypes or 'Sun Pictures', shown on the inside front cover of this book. Measuring 445 × 288 mm (17 ½ × 11 ½ inches), it was printed in red and blue ink with a range of display typefaces and a beautiful decorative border composed of intricate ornaments. Snare was a well-known jobbing printer who produced election material, theatre posters and general items. He also compiled the *Post Office Directory of Reading* (1842) and *Snare's Berkshire Guide* (1843) and ran a bookshop and library in Minster Street, Reading. He had a great interest in painting and sculpture and would certainly have been fascinated by the work of the Establishment. When time and budget allowed, Snare indulged in creating highly decorative designs printed in colour for his clients. Cowderoy was very proud of his commission and later commented:

The bill which I had printed to send out with parcels of pictures to the great houses all over the kingdom… . It was the work of the most aesthetic of printers (the late Mr. John Snare, of the Berkshire Library in Reading), and I do not think it could be excelled as an example of coloured typography even… today.

The work continues

Not long after the publication of Part 1 of *The Pencil of Nature* and while Henneman and his team were busy producing more prints for the following numbers, Talbot began work on his next project. In the autumn of 1844, Talbot had embarked on a tour of Scotland, ostensibly following in the footsteps of the great novelist, Sir Walter Scott, to photograph places associated with the writer and the settings of his books. Equipped with a number of cameras, Talbot took images of Abbotsford, Melrose Abbey, Doune Castle, Dryburgh Abbey, Heriot's Hospital and landscape views of Loch Katrine, as well as the monument to Scott erected in Edinburgh. Talbot selected 23 photographs to form a visual guidebook but provided no accompanying text other than a title page and list of contents, so the book was more of an album. Talbot gave it the title *Sun Pictures in Scotland*. It was published in July 1845 and sold at the price of one guinea. Although the edition was small – only 120 copies – it still meant that Henneman had to fulfil an order for 2760 prints while also working on *The Pencil of Nature*.

Talbot's precise aims and intentions in producing the book are uncertain. There was a growing demand for travel books as transportation became accessible to a wider range of the public; perhaps Talbot wanted to demonstrate again the potential of photography as book illustration. Talbot seems to have seen the book as an 'artistic' exercise and the images are certainly sensitive and carefully composed but also conservative and 'literal', lacking the romantic drama and power of Scott's imagination and description. However, mainly due to the persuasive skills of his mother, Lady Elizabeth, over 100 copies were sold, many to members of her wealthy and aristocratic circle. Subscribers included Queen Victoria, the Duke of Devonshire, Madame Lionel de Rothschild and Lord Dudley, as well as other collectors and calotype enthusiasts.

In 1846 another pioneering publication appeared: a small book containing only three photographic illustrations, entitled *The Talbotype Applied to Hieroglyphics*. The subject was an inscription on an ancient Egyptian tablet or 'stela' of King Sethos and his viceroy that had recently been rediscovered. Drawings of the inscription, the accompanying translation by Samuel Birch of the British Museum and hand-written notes had been photographed and prints made, probably by Henneman in Reading, and pasted into the book. Talbot himself might have funded the publication as he had a passionate interest in ancient languages. Again this modest publication had significance as a 'first': it was the first time photography was used in this field and it has since become

central to the practice of archaeology as a tool and method of recording the past.

The last publication to come out of the Reading Establishment was a volume of photographs of works of art that was an addition to three volumes written by the art historian William Stirling called the *Annals of the Artists of Spain*. This too was an important milestone – the first book published on fine art to be illustrated by photographs. In the field of art history, photography has since made it possible to see and appreciate art from around the world without having to travel.

Stirling was a scholar of independent means and had visited Spain on the 'Grand Tours' he undertook after leaving University. As part of his research for the book he had returned to Spain in 1845 and begun gathering material there and from collectors in Britain to use as illustrations. Stirling was himself a major collector of Spanish art and had already written three volumes of scholarly text that considered the wider social, cultural, religious and political context of each work. The text was illustrated, as was conventional, using steel- and wood-engraved copies of the work. However, the fourth volume contained sixty-six photographs commissioned from the Reading Establishment. Fifty copies of this volume were produced for private circulation. The subject matter included paintings, drawings, sculpture and prints as well as a number of architectural designs and book illustrations; the artists included El Greco, Velazquez, Murillo and Goya.

Henneman took the photographs under the guidance of Stirling. The possibility of travelling far to take photographs of the work was limited and the need for daylight was also a serious restriction – photography inside museums and galleries was almost impossible, and there was a limit to what could be brought to Reading. In the event, most of the photographs taken were of engravings, etchings, lithographs after oil paintings, painted copies or drawings after the original. It is not surprising that they tried to avoid taking photographs of original oil paintings as they would have encountered the same problems we have today – light reflecting off the varnish covering the painting, and rendering accurately the tonal variations and colours of a painting in a monochrome photograph.

Henneman experienced problems with completing all the pictures for the *Annals of the Artists of Spain* due to the weather. On 5 May 1847 he expressed his frustrations in a letter to Talbot:

> I have finished the principal order for Mr Sterling [Stirling]. I intended to finish to day but the weather turned out very bad, and altho I copied some they are not to my satisfaction being convinced I can do them a <u>great</u> deal better, especially two Oil paintings Mr Sterling wanted me to do to see how we could do oil painting, as he has a great many to do, please to let me kno if the glass house curtains are up, for if so, <u>in case</u> the weather should be bad to morrow, I think I better bring them up to finish in London, if the weather proofs fine tomorrow I can finish the <u>whole</u> lot, except one wich is 4 feet 6 inch by 2ft 2 inch and he wants it diminished to 3 inch by 1 ½, I should very much you to let me kno <u>how</u> to do it I think the best way to get it <u>distinct</u> is to take a large one first <u>and then</u> a small one from that…

Stirling explained in his preface to the volume his objectives in commissioning this special edition using 'the beautiful photographic process invented by Mr. Fox Talbot'; he hoped that 'if it should induce abler contributors to the history of art to illustrate their works by the pencil of nature, – my end will be achieved, and my labour amply rewarded'. Stirling clearly appreciated the wider applications of photography, not just for documenting and preserving works of art, but also for making them available to the general public and future generations.

Sadly, as with so many of the mass-produced photographs from the Reading Establishment, these too suffered from fading and discolouration, undermining the hope for permanence.

While working for Stirling on the *Annals*, Henneman had also been very busy taking portraits of a number of local figures, including George Lovejoy and Mary Russell Mitford. On 5 May 1847 he wrote to Talbot:

> ... the peopel are all highly delighted with their Portraits and every body has seen them wanted theirs done, <u>I suppose</u> you could not let me kno by return of post what you sel the <u>exclusive</u> Licence for Berkshire for – likewise... will you sel the Copyright of Miss Mitfords Portrait, and what prise do you want for it, I should feel much obliged if you could let me kno these two questions by return of post.

Miss Mitford was a Reading celebrity and a national literary figure: a poet, playwright and the author of two very popular books of the time. *Our Village* was a series of sketches of village life and local characters based on the hamlet of Three Mile Cross outside Reading, where she had a cottage; it was published in five volumes between 1824 and 1832. *Belford Regis*, a thinly disguised and idealised sketch of the neighbourhood and society of Reading, was published in 1835. Later in the nineteenth century it became a popular pastime to collect little *carte-de-visite* portraits of famous people, and Henneman seems to have anticipated this trend. He took the portrait of Miss Mitford on 20 April 1847. Writing to Talbot from Reading, he described the event:

> ... the celebrated Authoress, Miss Mitford, came to day and I got her to sit for her portrait, wish came out very fine considering her age [Miss Mitford was 61], I think the

Photographic portrait of Mary Russell Mitford

(1787—1855)

negative is worth <u>at least</u> 25 pounds. She begged of me to take her dog, (well knowing in most all her works) to <u>please her</u> I took him, not of course expecting he would remain quit and more over bing all one colour (Dark brown) but wonderful to State he remained for 4 minutes as still as if he was dead, so I got a fine negative of him also, I took about 20 portraits to day of diferent people and was very sucsesful on the whole – Mr Lovejoy told me he can get me at least 50 sitters if I would open here for a fortnight before going to London and the Editor of the Mercury [the *Reading Mercury* newspaper] (whose portrait I likewise took) promised me a paragraph in his paper if I could do it...

Compared to the Daguerreotype, Talbot's calotype still needed a long exposure time which made it less attractive for taking portraits. The sitter had to concentrate and remain perfectly still for up to a minute, and often a head clamp was used, hidden from the camera at the back of the head – no wonder this frequently resulted in a strained expression on the sitter's face. But Henneman was anxious to develop this side of the business as he saw its huge potential. He wanted to concentrate on portraiture in the premises in Reading but unfortunately Talbot and Cowderoy had other ideas. They had decided to move the Establishment to London and were actively seeking suitable premises in the city.

The end of the Establishment

Looking back on these momentous days it is natural to focus on the technological advances and the great publications of the Reading Establishment, and it is easy to lose sight of the fact that these were the everyday occupations of a group of ordinary individuals; for them it was their work, carried out in the context of daily life with all its difficulties and personal tensions. It certainly was not an idyll. As we will see, there were financial problems; no doubt there were also clashes of personality; and often, as one might expect with such experimental work, things went wrong. Life was not easy and the work not always pleasurable – behind it all there were human stories.

In July 1846, at a time of great activity at the Establishment, Henneman married. Always a popular character, particularly with the ladies, he had decided to settle down – but why did he choose to take on such responsibilities at that point in time? Had he fallen hopelessly in love? He must have had faith in the possibility of making a sufficiently good living from photography to support a family. His bride was Sarah Price, one of the housemaids at Lacock Abbey. Perhaps it was a long-term relationship that had begun when Henneman was a valet at Lacock.

Only a few months after the wedding, Sarah fell terribly ill and almost died. In a letter of 26 September 1846, Henneman wrote to Talbot from Oswestry, where Sarah seems to have been visiting friends:

I am sory to inform you that my wife is very ill With an attack of Englis Cohlera so violent that her life was disspared of, but I am happy to Say the doctors have pronounced her out off danger now. I riceved a letter, the Same day I wrote to you in Liverpool, of course I Started off to Oswestry imediately and have been here ever since, as I could not leave her; as she is getting better I intend leaving here the beginning off nex week, as she will not be able to leave here for at least a month so the atack has weakened her, She can hardly Speak, thiss Cholera is reigning very much in thiss part off the Country and Several people have died of it, I have been very poorly my Self but I think is was from fright and fatigue, but I am gust well again, and my Wife is thank god recovering fast how luckey She is with her kind friends...

Sarah could have just as easily have caught the illness in Reading. Although improvements had been made to lighting, paving and street sweeping in Reading, the main health problem in the town was the lack of a clean water supply and proper provision for dealing with sewage and drainage. In the 1840s, prominent Reading citizens (including George Lovejoy) began to campaign for improvements; public protest became frequent and enquiries were held, with evidence taken from members of the medical profession. It was reported that the worst affected areas were the crowded courts and backstreets of the town – some of the very streets and courts that Talbot passed on his way to the Establishment – where a large proportion of the poorer folk lived, packed into overcrowded houses close to open cesspools, foul privies and stinking pigsties. These areas were breeding grounds for disease: some people used communal taps that worked for only a few hours a day, others drew water from wells that were often contaminated, or from the river. Outbreaks of cholera, typhoid fever, smallpox and scarlatina were common. This was the reality of everyday life for Henneman and his team in Reading.

Hennemann's wife Sarah survived this first illness but sadly died shortly after, in 1848. But tragedy had struck Talbot too, for Lady Elizabeth, Talbot's mother, died in 1846. She had been an enthusiastic supporter of her son and his inventions and had played a crucial role in persuading Talbot to bring photography to the wider public. He greatly mourned her loss.

Relationships between Talbot and the staff at the Establishment were not always amicable. Talbot was engaged in many activities and the diversions that life in society demanded at Lacock and in London, and he was always researching and making new experiments; perhaps he sometimes failed to appreciate the situation of Henneman and his staff in Reading. For them, the Establishment was their living and the only source of income.

Henneman's terms and conditions of employment and the relationship with Talbot seem to have been confused. The income to pay for part of his wages and for staff wages, rent and running costs appears to have been generated by charging Talbot for each print produced (thus fluctuating according to output); but he also seems to have been paid a salary and Talbot covered some expenses – so was Henneman an independent manager of the business, in effect operating as a franchise, or was he an employee of Talbot's, running the business on his behalf?

How Henneman reacted when Talbot appointed Cowderoy is uncertain. Was he offended or bitter by an outsider being given a major role in the enterprise which he must have felt was his own, or was he relieved to be spared the burden of administration and promotion so that he could concentrate on taking photographs and producing prints? Things were falling apart for Henneman – he found that Harrison had been put in charge of printing (at which he was very competent) so Henneman must have felt even more that his position was being undermined.

Perhaps because of the impending wedding, Henneman wanted to re-negotiate his agreement of terms with Talbot and Cowderoy approached Talbot on his behalf. On 30 April 1846, Cowderoy wrote to Talbot and, after a preamble concerning other matters, took up Henneman's case:

I should have written to you Tuesday Evening but I was obliged to meet Mr Sergt. Talfourd and other Gentlemen preparatory to the annual Meeting of our Institution which was held in the Evening and on which occasion I resigned my Secretaryship finding it interfered too much with business.

I have again talked matters over with Henneman who has been giving me evidences of the disasters and casualties (– certainly not trifling) which are to be set off against his profit on the pictures. He complains of his present position, having engaged Harrison and two lads in the expectation that we were about to make a considerable Stock. However, without troubling you with his grievances, the following he submits and seems very firm and decided against any modification of the terms – vizt – If he continues to make the pictures and supply them at the present rates he requires that he shall not make less than an <u>average</u> of 400 weekly during the year – that when engaged in taking negatives he shall be paid 10/- per day and travelling expenses including 5/- per day towards tavern bills – Or secondly – If he is to be paid by Salary he asks for £150 per Annum and 10 pr Cent on Net profits of the business – or if you prefer it – instead of the per Centage – 1/- per hundred sheets of <u>good</u> positives and 1/- for each good negative which you approve. Travelling expenses and 5/- towards Tavern bills when from home. The rent and taxes to be paid by you as well as all other expenses of the business and he will occupy the house if you wish it paying you £15 per annum as Rent. His present Stock of fittings, Apparatus, Chemicals &^{c} to be paid for by you. He also requires that he shall have an engagement for 2 years, teaching whom you please a general knowledge of the Art, but if he is required to reveal <u>everything</u> he knows, he then asks for a three years engagement. If neither of these proposals are acceded to he expresses his intention of leaving but offers before doing so to teach anyone you may require for £10.

You misunderstood him in supposing that he had any objection to my supervision of his Establishment. His vexation was the result of your determination to limit the making of positives. I hope we shall come to some conclusion which will retain Henneman as I foresee a great uncertainty of meeting with another person so suitable in all aspects…

These conditions, as expressed by Cowderoy, seem very demanding in tone and far from the mutual respect, friendship and easy relationship between Talbot and Henneman in previous years. Talbot did agree with Henneman's conditions and signed a three-year contract with him on 6 June 1846, but perhaps he was upset by Cowderoy's intervention or realised that Cowderoy had taken advantage of Henneman's and his own absence from Reading during their time of bereavement. For whatever reason, the relationship between Cowderoy and Talbot became strained – so much so that on 14 December 1846, Cowderoy wrote a frank reply to a letter from Talbot and outlined his situation:

Your letter of this morning has put beyond a doubt my former opinion of your intention (viz') to get rid of me so soon as it suited your convenience. It is useless blinking the matter and I must therefore beg to be excused for speaking plainly The fact of our Agreement for two years altho' you never fulfilled your promise of signing a specific Agreement in Writing, is yet amply attested and I can legally insist on its performance but as I have no wish to thrust myself or my services on any one to whom either would be unpalatable so I am willing to forego any claim to another years Engagement provided I am dealt with fairly & honourable. I shall have [illegible deletion] earned very hardly my £100 by the end of the first year and if I were to consent to be turned suddenly adrift without notice, after having sacrificed a part of my own business to enter into this I should be doing myself a manifest injustice In all fairness therefore I should require some compensation but do not wish to be dictating terms or indeed to be chargeable with acting in any way offensively or disrespectfully but I have duties which I owe to myself and my Children as well as to others and must beg to add that I trust your dealings with me in future will be characterized by candour and plain speaking...

In his reply to this letter, Talbot denied Cowderoy's claim that he wished to dismiss him, but Cowderoy did leave the Establishment that year.

It became clear that despite all the hard work put in by Henneman and his staff, the set-up in Reading was losing money, and Talbot's plans for moving the business to London were becoming a reality. In a letter of 27 January 1846, Cowderoy had provided an estimate of the outlay needed for the first year of establishing a new photographic business. It included figures for rent, furniture and fittings, apparatus and equipment, fixed salaries, advertising and travelling expenses and so on; interestingly, it mentions costs for publishing a 'handbook' on photography which never appeared. His estimate total was £1200. Cowderoy calculated:

Of this I estimate one third (−£400) as the actual amount required as a new Investment, as a large portion of the above Items would not be called for until returns were obtained to meet them.

If the project is but moderately successful the above sum must be realised by the end of a year in addition to which there would be in hand Stock and Materials for future operations without the necessity for a further outlay. If the Establishment

Henneman's business card

but pays its expenses the first year it must yield a good profit in future years.

In December 1846, premises were found in London at 122 Regent Street at an annual rent of £130. The landlord was a John Newman, who was an instrument maker and had a workshop on the premises. The intention was to build a studio on the roof of the building to make best use of the daylight. Talbot still had faith in Henneman and had decided to back him in setting up a photographic portrait business. Claudet's agreement with Talbot for the rights to use the calotype process in London had lapsed and he had returned to exclusively making Daguerreotypes, so the way was clear for the new enterprise.

For a while both businesses operated in tandem. Henneman set about running the Reading establishment down and finishing outstanding work; at the same time he started to organise the new business, decorating the studio and darkrooms and fitting them out for the opening.

During these last days, Talbot was travelling abroad and so for a short time he appointed another Reading man with business experience, Mr Tobias S. Telfer, to keep an eye on things and take over from Cowderoy. Talbot had asked his friend the Reverend Calvert Jones, another practitioner of photography, to oversee things in his absence and possibly run the business in London, but Jones had declined the offer. He had been very active in supporting Henneman in his opposition to the move to London. He wrote to Talbot in December 1846 reporting that he had great faith in the abilities of both Harrison and Henneman but warned Talbot of Cowderoy: 'Mr. Cowderoy has evidently throughout behaved very ill to you, and seems to have erred in almost every thing which he has touched, and I shd certainly pack him off unreservedly.' As we have seen, Talbot acted quickly in dismissing Cowderoy.

Calvert Jones and another friend, the Reverend George Bridges, had been regular visitors and helpers at Reading; indeed, Henneman had made prints from their negatives for sale. At one time Talbot had intended to include prints by these colleagues in *The Pencil of Nature* but, as we have seen, his ambitions for the book had been cut back. In 1845, Calvert Jones and Bridges had joined Talbot's cousin, Kit Talbot, on a tour of the Mediterranean to take calotype negatives which were sent back to Henneman in Reading to print. As part of the trip they visited Malta and probably established the contact there that was later followed up by Cowderoy.

By the autumn of 1847, the business in Regent Street, now given the name 'Sun Picture Rooms', was fully operational and the Reading Establishment had closed. Although it had lasted for only three years and was a failure as a commercial enterprise, it marked a pivotal moment in the development of photography and helped to shape how we live our lives today.

Talbot's aim – to prove that photography could change the world of publishing and book illustration – had been fulfilled in principle but not in practice. His photographic processes were wonderfully successful when producing prints in limited quantities with the care and attention he could give to individual prints in the ideal conditions at Lacock Abbey. Mass production involving the making of thousands of prints under pressure was another matter; it proved to be overambitious and had exposed weaknesses. The demands of commercialisation inevitably led to a loss of quality and permanence. With daily production targets to meet, Henneman could not wait for perfect weather conditions and was often forced to work on days of weak light, which meant loss of tonal strength and made the prints more likely to fade. There were days when chemicals were troublesome and fixing prints properly was a continual issue. Sir John Herschel's discovery of 'hypo' had many advantages but it required thorough washing to remove it from the paper after fixing. This demanded copious quantities of clean water, and we have seen that in Reading at this time the water supply was very poor, often limited to a few hours a day and badly polluted. Heating the water to the right temperature was essential to the process and very costly. It is hardly surprising that the staff at the Establishment were forced to cut corners to keep up with production – with the result that the prints were not always washed adequately.

Talbot was aware of the problems of fading and discolouration that had been so publicly demonstrated by the 7000 free prints distributed in the *Art-Union*, and he must have been alarmed that the prints in *The Pencil of Nature* were also beginning to deteriorate. These were truly embarrassing failings that undermined the reputation of his process.

Producing photographic prints in quantity to be pasted into books proved to be impractical, although with further advances it was done on a limited scale throughout the nineteenth century. But Talbot had been working for some while on practical ways to use photography for reproducing images using traditional printer's inks and presses. In 1852 he took out a patent on a process that involved coating a metal plate with light-sensitised gelatine and exposing it through a photographic negative; as with the traditional etching process, the exposed material resisted the biting of acid in degrees relative to the amount of exposure to light through the negative. This was the origin of what has become known as 'photogravure', and Talbot spent much of the rest of his life perfecting this process, which he called 'photoglyphic engraving'. In the twentieth century, photogravure developed into a major industrial printing process, mainly used in magazine printing.

During his experiments, Talbot encountered problems with large, flat areas of one tone holding ink unevenly and middle tones reproducing poorly. His solution stemmed from earlier photogenic drawings he had made using cloth. He observed that layers of fabric, especially the loose weave of gauze, created a grid of tiny dots when exposed. He realised that if applied to the surface of a printing plate, the printed dots, and the white areas around them, would be perceived as gradated tones or tints of grey by the human eye. In the patent of 1852, Talbot explained: 'To produce the effect of engraved line or of uniform shading, the image of a folded piece of gauze, or other suitable material, is impressed upon the gelatine prior to the image of the object required being formed'. He called this effect 'photographic screens' or 'veils'. In fact he had invented the principle of the 'half-tone' process, which has become the main way of printing continuous tone photographs right up to the present day – look through a magnifying glass at the photographs in your book, magazine or newspaper and you will see dots of varying size, larger dots producing darker areas, small dots light areas.

Postscript

So what happened to the staff of the Establishment after its closure? Henneman was put in charge of the business in Regent Street, which flourished in the early years. Talbot had generously provided Henneman with the licence for London and paid for the conversion and fitting out of the premises and for the rent for the first two years, but he made it clear that he wanted no liability or active participation in the business.

Thomas Malone, Alfred Harrison and his younger brother David went to join Henneman in London. John Henderson stayed in Reading and pursued another career. Thomas Malone was a very talented and expert chemist and Talbot took advantage of his skills by involving him in his experiments, but Malone also formed a partnership with Henneman and went on to become a photographer of note. Their business received a considerable boost when Henneman was appointed 'Photographer Ordinary to Her Majesty' – Talbot's half-sister Caroline, who was a Lady in Waiting, had recommended him to Queen Victoria. The Great Exhibition of 1851 was a popular showcase for the new art of photography and Henneman and Malone gained a large amount of work through exhibiting there. Both men worked hard to expand the business, but growing competition and new developments such as the wet collodion process invented by Fredrick Scott Archer slowly brought about the decline of their enterprise. By 1857 it had failed. Eventually Henneman ended up as an assistant to a photographer in Birmingham, but his health suffered after years of exposure to the conditions in photographic dark rooms. He had married again and had children, but he ended his days running a lowly boarding house – a sad demise for a man with such talents and aspirations.

Cowderoy returned to his previous business in Reading, moving premises to Castle Street, until he emigrated to

Melbourne, Australia, in 1853. He became a very successful businessman and a pillar of society in Melbourne; he founded the Chamber of Commerce and eventually became Mayor of St Kilda. In later life, Cowderoy published a number of articles on his experiences of early photography, always praising Talbot and supporting his claim to the invention; he seems not to have held a grudge.

After the closure of the Reading Establishment, Talbot continued to work on photography and in particular on developing photoglyphic engraving but, always a visionary, he found a new enthusiasm in experimenting with 'motive power'. As usual, he took out a number of patents and designed some ingenious engines – electric motors, internal combustion engines and engines that derived power from 'rapid expansion' due to the application of extreme cold and heat. He also outlined ideas for wind and water turbine engines and designs for an 'Atmospheric railway'.

In 1847 a photographic club was founded which is sometimes referred to as the 'Calotype Club'. Distinguished members included Roger Fenton, who was to become famous for his images of the Crimean War, and Frederick Scott Archer, who in 1851 invented the next revolutionary step in the development of photography – the wet collodion process. Throughout the late 1840s and 1850s, Talbot had engaged in unpopular disputes over his insistence on enforcing his restrictive patents, much criticised in the press; now he tried to claim that Scott Archer's process was covered by his patent, but in a dramatic trial in 1854 he lost the case. The wet collodion process became free to the world and quickly took over as the dominant method of photography. Talbot did not bother to renew his patent.

Towards the end of his life Talbot became more of a recluse, but his studies continued; mathematics, his passion for translating ancient cuneiform inscriptions and running his house and estate at Lacock filled his time.

Even after Henneman's move to London, Lovejoy's remained an outlet for calotype prints or 'Sun Pictures'. Tobias Telfer wrote to Talbot on 8 November 1847 from 122 Regent Street and mentioned that Lovejoy was behind with his payments:

A Camera &c is now ready for the Surgeon of the 1ˢᵗ Regᵗ Life Guards, who I expect will be here this week to take instructions ere proceeding to India, this Gent. was recommended by an officer in the same Regiment who had his instructions and Camera &c about a fortnight back, this latter Gent was brought here by Lord Beresford –

Lovejoy has not yet paid; Malone asked for the money when last in Reading, the answer was that Lovejoy will be in Town in a few days, this is the same as he told Harrison about six weeks back. I think that should Lovejoy require more sun Pictures at any future period, that he be made to pay Cash for them deducting one third ...

Much later, in 1854, Lovejoy was still in contact with Talbot himself, inquiring after licences on behalf of a young friend he was trying to help:

I was in town a few days ago and spoke to Mr Hennemann [sic] about a friend of mine here who has been making some attempts in Photography and succeeding so well as to induce him to think of making a business of it and applying to you for a License for the use of your Patent in Reading His friends have heard that a trial is pending and advises him to wait – In the mean time however he wishes me to ask to kindly favor me with your terms for a License for this neighbourhood.

Knowing the benevolence of your disposition I may just perhaps say that he is just the young man you will be pleased to assist – as in the first place there is no doubt of his turning out pictures that will not disgrace your beautiful discovery and in the next place he has lost all his property (between 2 & 3,000£) by being deceived in a partnership (a Paper Mills) into which he entered – since which he has been engaged professionally in mounting Microscopic Objects but obliged to give it up on account of his Eyes suffering – He finds Photography just suits him...

But Lovejoy had not remained exclusively loyal to Talbot's process. Sometime in the 1850s he published an advertisement sheet notifying the Reading public that a 'Mr Barber of Winchester', who described himself as an 'Artist in Daguerreotype', would be building a temporary 'commodious glass room' at his premises in London Street and open for a short period to take portraits. There follows a rather extravagant description of the wonders of photographic portraiture:

Among the many discoveries and applications of modern science, there are none perhaps more interesting than Photography. The Man of Science regards it as one of the proudest triumphs of later days, that the fleeting and evanescent form of one of the most subtle agents of nature, Light, should be arrested in its course, and rendered permanent – the Connoisseur views it as an unexpected but invaluable means of producing the most faultless representations of nature and art; and persons in general are induced to regard it with peculiar interest in supplying them with more faithful memorials of those that are near and dear to them, than by any other human agency can be produced, as by this means parents and children, relatives and friends may retain each others beaming eyes and glowing countenances, with all individual peculiarities, painted by Nature's own pencil – when distance or death has separated them...

Specimens may be seen, with card of terms, at Mr. Lovejoy's, Bookseller, Reading.

... Printed Hints to subjects respecting Dress, before sitting for a Photographic Portrait, may be had at Mr. Lovejoy's...

After the closure of the Reading Establishment and as the public became more familiar with photography, an increasing number of photographers opened up studios in Reading as well as in many other towns in the country. One family firm, Francis Dann, opened in Broad Street in 1856 and later generations ran the business until 1939. Although the name 'Francis Dann' was over the door of the premises, it was in fact his wife, Frances, who had set up the business. It was said that she had learnt the art of photography from a travelling salesman and had taught her husband the process. Surely this must make her one of the first female professional photographers in the country?

In *Macaulay's Reading Directory* for 1859, eight photographers are listed as working in the town. By 1900, *Smith's Directory of Reading* lists 15. Walton Adams opened his photographic studios in Reading in 1886; his son, Marcus Adams, went on to become a celebrated photographer who took portraits of many famous people, including the Royal Family. In turn, his son Gilbert carried on the business and trained Peter Grugeon (1918–80), who later also became a Royal photographer. Grugeon took a portrait of the present Queen in 1975 that later inspired the American artist Andy Warhol to use it as the basis for a series of screen prints.

HERE
W·H·FOX TALBOT F·R·S
Father of Modern Photography
CONDUCTED HIS
READING ESTABLISHMENT
1844 – 5

Talbot House

Plaques on the house at 55 Baker Street
(the date is incorrect – it should read 1844 –7)

Standing in front of the building once occupied by the Reading Establishment one hundred and seventy years after it opened, there is little to remind you of its significance in the history of photography other than two plaques, one a modest commemorative plaque, the other the building name.

The road has been renamed: it is now part of Baker Street and the house number is 55. The street is lined with cars and in the distance you are aware of the hum of the traffic on

55 Baker Street today (originally 8 Russell Terrace)

Reading's inner distribution road, a concrete canyon that slices through the town. In recent years the outbuildings and yard have been used by a building firm – nothing at the rear resembles the famous photograph taken by Talbot. The house itself has been turned into flats and bedsits, with the inevitable row of wheelie bins lining up outside on the pavement.

It is sad to reflect that this site of events that were of world importance is now neglected and virtually forgotten. Still, Reading should celebrate the connections with William Henry Fox Talbot and the role that the Establishment has in the story of photography: it is a great part of our town's history.

Notes and sources

A mysterious gentleman

Extracts from John Henderson's letters are quoted from the following article, which has been a major source: Snow, V.F. and Thomas, D.B., 'The Talbotype Establishment at Reading 1844–1847', *The Photographic Journal*, vol. 106, no. 2, 1966, 56–67.

The birth of photography

Background information on the Diorama is from Hyde, R., *Panoramania*, London: Trefoil Publications Ltd and Barbican Art Gallery, 1988.

Quotations from Talbot's own account of his discoveries come from his introductory remarks in *The Pencil of Nature*, London: Longman, Brown, Green and Longmans, 1844.

The description of Talbot's improved process is quoted from Gernsheim, Helmut and Alison, *A Concise History of Photography*, London: Thames and Hudson, 1965, p. 31.

Quotes from letters between Talbot and Herschel are taken from Buckland, Gail, *Fox Talbot and the Invention of Photography*, London: Scolar Press, 1980, pp. 65–66.

Photography comes to Reading

The timetable for Talbot's journey to Reading and details of his walk to Russell Terrace are based on *The Post-Office Reading Directory*, Reading: John Snare, 1842.

General sources on the railway and social conditions in Reading include Phillips, D., *The Story of Reading*, Newbury: Countryside Books, revised edition 2004; and Sowan, A., *All Change at Reading: The railway and the station 1840–2013*, Reading: Two Rivers Press, 2013.

Articles and letters concerning the dispute between Havell and Talbot have been published in Buckland, Gail, *Fox Talbot and the Invention of Photography*, London: Scolar Press, 1980, p. 50–52. See also *William Havell 1782–1857*, catalogue to an exhibition held at Reading Museum & Art Gallery in 1981, with an introduction by Felicity Owen.

Kit Talbot's letter to his cousin can be found at http://foxtalbot.dmu.ac.uk (Doc. No. 6859), where ten thousand letters from and to Talbot have been made available online through a project initiated by the University of Glasgow and now hosted by De Montford University. The correspondence editor is Professor Larry Schaaf.

At work in the Establishment

Extracts from John Henderson's letters are quoted from Snow, V.F. and Thomas, D.B., 'The Talbotype Establishment at Reading 1844–1847', *The Photographic Journal*, vol. 106, no. 2, 1966, 56–67.

The letter from Henneman to Talbot can be found at http://foxtalbot.dmu.ac.uk (Doc. No. 5005).

The Pencil of Nature

A major source of quotations and general information for this chapter is Schaaf, Larry J., *The Pencil of Nature, Anniversary Facsimile: Introductory Volume*, New York: Hans P. Kraus, Jr. Inc., 1989, and Talbot's introductory remarks and notes on the prints in *The Pencil of Nature*.

The extract from Talbot's letter to Herschel is quoted from Buckland, Gail, *Fox Talbot and the Invention of Photography*, London: Scolar Press, 1980. Talbot's letter to William Snow Harris is quoted from http://foxtalbot.dmu.ac.uk (Doc. No. 4740).

A day in the life of the Establishment

The technical details of the processes are based on an account written by Thomas Malone and published in the 'Amateurs' Column' of *The Liverpool and Manchester Photographic Journal*, vol. 1, 1857, 270.

Reception and promotion

Quotations from reviews and newspaper articles are taken from Buckland, Gail, *Fox Talbot and the Invention of Photography*, London: Scolar Press, 1980; Schaaf, Larry J., *The Pencil of Nature, Anniversary Facsimile: Introductory Volume*, New York: Hans P. Kraus, Jr. Inc., 1989; Snow, V.F. and Thomas, D.B., 'The Talbotype Establishment at Reading 1844–1847', *The Photographic Journal*, vol. 106, no. 2, 1966, 56–67; or they are directly from the *Reading Mercury*.

The letters of Henneman and Cowderoy are quoted from the correspondence made available at http://foxtalbot.dmu.ac.uk (Doc. Nos 5167, 5640, 5690).

Cowderoy's remarks on the Snare poster are quoted from Schaaf, Larry J., *Sun Pictures, from Talbot to Turner*, Catalogue Fifteen, New York: Hans P. Kraus, Jr. Fine Photographs, 2003.

The work continues

Quotations from letters are taken from the correspondence at http://foxtalbot.dmu.ac.uk (Doc. Nos 5936, 5924).

The end of the Establishment

Quotations from letters are taken from the correspondence at http://foxtalbot.dmu.ac.uk (Doc. Nos 5736, 5640, 5802, 5537).

Details of 'photographic screens' or 'veils' are based on Schaaf, Larry J., *Sun Pictures, Talbot and Photogravure*, Catalogue Twelve, New York: Hans P. Kraus, Jr. Fine Photographs, 2003.

Postscript

Quotations from letters are taken from the correspondence at http://foxtalbot.dmu.ac.uk (Doc. Nos 6045, 6954).

A copy of Lovejoy's advertisement can be found pasted into one of his scrapbooks held in the collections of the Local Studies Library at Reading Central Library. Details of local photographers are from Reading street directories and from Southerton, Mary, *A Century of Photography in Reading*, unpublished manuscript, 1986 (a copy is available in the Local Studies Library at Reading Central Library).

General sources

Arnold, H.J.P., *William Henry Fox Talbot: Pioneer of photography and man of science*, London: Hutchinson, 1977.

Batchen, Geoffrey, *William Henry Fox Talbot*, London: Phaidon Press Ltd, 2008.

Buckland, Gail, *Fox Talbot and the Invention of Photography*, London: Scolar Press, 1980.

Gernsheim, Helmut and Alison, *A Concise History of Photography*, London: Thames and Hudson, 1965.

Hannavy, John, *Fox Talbot*, 3rd edition, Oxford: Shire Publications Ltd, 1997.

Jammes, André, *William H. Fox Talbot: Inventor of the negative–positive process*, New York: Collier Books, 1972.

Lassam, Robert, *Fox Talbot: Photographer*, Tisbury: The Compton Press Ltd, 1979.

Schaaf, Larry J., *The Pencil of Nature, Anniversary Facsimile: Introductory Volume*, New York: Hans P. Kraus, Jr. Inc., 1989.

Schaaf, Larry J., *The Photographic Art of William Fox Talbot*, Princeton: Princeton University Press, 2000.

Schaaf, Larry J., *Sun Pictures, Talbot and Photogravure*, Catalogue Twelve, New York: Hans P. Kraus, Jr. Fine Photographs, 2003.

Schaaf, Larry J., *Sun Pictures, from Talbot to Turner*, Catalogue Fifteen, New York: Hans P. Kraus, Jr. Fine Photographs, 2003.

Snow, V.F. and Thomas, D.B., 'The Talbotype Establishment at Reading 1844–1847', *The Photographic Journal*, vol. 106, no. 2, 1966, 56–67.

Watson, Roger and Rappaport, Helen, *Capturing the Light*, London: Macmillan, 2013.

Two Rivers Press has been publishing in and about Reading since 1994. Founded by the artist Peter Hay (1951–2003), the press continues to delight readers, local and further afield, with its varied list of individually designed, thought-provoking books.